On Being a Fulfilled Catholic Priest

Understanding the Experience of Meaning and Meaninglessness in the Priesthood

CORNELIUS UCHE OKEKE

To
Ron Brosofske
&
Wanda Edie

Cornelius Uche Okeke

TABLE OF CONTENT

Cornelius Uche Okeke

Presentation

Henri Bergson's philosophical system aimed at an attack upon reason and intellect. He felt that this faculty did not give a comprehensive insight into life. A cornfield, for instance, could not be described by pulling a grain of maize, placing it on a paper and showing it to students. It was a crack down on analysis which smashes human beings as if they were mere atoms.

Psychologists, however, have recognized and confirmed the biblical insight into the depths of the human mind, namely, that within every human being is a conflict of the law of the Spirit and the law of the flesh. Fr. Cornelius describes it as "conflict of inclinations", "no human being is completely present to him/herself". They have tried to develop a synthesis between the discordant and battling forces inside human beings.

This is the type of work Fr. Cornelius as a psychologist and Catholic priest tried to achieve in this *On Being a Fulfilled Catholic Priest*, appropriating the gains of sociology and psychology within the periscope of the ecclesial teachings, to analyze who a priest is and who he is called to become in order to be so fulfilled and to share in the accompanying joy of such witness of life.

I recommend this book to all priests and seminarians, as well as those engaged in any religious ministry, who seek meaning to their lives and vocations.

Fr. Cyril Udebunu (Ph.D)
Pope John Paul II Major Seminary
Okpuno, Awka.

Foreword

The search for meaning in life is very deep in the heart of every human person, since such a meaning sustains life and enables one to carry on irrespective of the difficulties along the way. When such a meaning is lacking, despair, depression and frustration can set in and these can sometimes lead to suicide when one no longer sees the reason to go on living.

Fr. Cornelius Okeke, a scholar and a psychologist has taken time to explore this fundamental search in life with regard to the Catholic priesthood. He convincingly argues that everyone makes a sense of his own vocation in life. One needs to make conscious efforts to find meaning in one's life since devoid of meaning life is not worth living. When one's life has meaning, one enjoys living. On the contrary, when one's life loses its meaning, one feels depressed and feels there is nothing worth living for anymore. This is why this can sometimes result in the ugly incident of suicide.

This is what Camus in his book *The Myth of Sisyphus* means when he says: "the meaning of life is the most urgent of questions". Examining the reason for suicide, he says that absurdity is what leads people to take their life. He defines absurdity as a disparity between two terms that are supposed to be joined by harmony or causality but in fact are disjoined. The absurd is an affront to reason. It is essentially a divorce between man and his life. Fox argues that Camus' concept of absurd rhymes with Qoheleth's concept of *hebel* (vanity). One's life needs to have a meaning before one can enjoy living.

In the light of the above, Fr. Cornelius explores all the avenues which enable priests to find deep and lasting meaning in their priestly vocation. Prominent among them is the intimacy with Christ. It is union with Christ that leads a priest to discover his true identity and the meaning of his priesthood. Thus, a priest needs to have a personal experience, a personal knowledge of Jesus Christ, since a priest's identity is deeply rooted in the person of Christ and His mission. It was such intimacy with Christ which sustained all the apostles in their ministry. Communion with Jesus facilitates the ongoing conversion in the life of every priest. It enables him to make the right decisions and choices. The more right decisions are made on daily basis, the easier the subsequent ones become. Union with Christ enhances the bridging of the gap between the ideal self and the real self. It enables a priest to make a total gift of himself to God without reservation. It enables him to live out the three evangelical counsels of poverty, chastity and obedience without interpreting them to his own convenience. He does not see the counsels as being there just to enhance his priestly ministry but he sees them as rooted in the life and person of Christ whom he is called to emulate. If a priest is united with Christ, he finds his true security in God and not in shares and economic investment and affluence.

Unless a priest finds the meaning of his priesthood in Christ, he faces the danger of identity crisis, dissatisfaction and emotional breakdown, since it is this union with Christ which defines the identity of every priest. The need for prayer in the life of a priest cannot be overemphasized. Prayer is like the umbilical chord that unites a priest to God.

Union with Jesus brings about vocational maturity which enables a priest to know the conscious and subconscious motivations inherent in his life so that he is able to bring harmony between his needs, desires, wants crying out for gratification and the Gospel values. Such a priest is able to make sense of the tension between who he is and who he is called to be, and consequently become more integrated each day of his life.

When one speaks from his heart, other hearts are touched and transformed. What makes this work very interesting and very unique is that Fr. Cornelius is not just narrating what he read or learned from books, rather he shares his personal experience. the book is like a heart to heart talk which is the reason it has the power to make a great impression and to transform its readers. Cornelius' style of writing is such that when you begin to read you do not want to drop until you finish. I recommend this book to every priest, every seminarian, every aspirant and in fact to every Christian.

Fr. Victor Onwukeme, MSP
Rector
The National Missionary Seminary of St. Paul
Gwagwalada –

Prologue: Confession of God's Abiding Love

What follows in these pages have been largely informed by my experiences these past fifteen years as a Catholic priest. Though the content appears to be heavily researched, evidenced from the citations and notes, many aspects of it resonate with my lived experiences and those of the priests with whom I have shared my worries, joys, satisfactions, doubts, insights, and anxious search for the central ground of my life as a priest. The content also reflects my observations from encounters among us priests. In a way, this book is a personal testimony of the experience of God as a tremendous lover, and of the beauty and joy of the Catholic priesthood lived from the depth of personal relationship with God in Jesus Christ through the Holy Spirit. It is also an acknowledgement that this love relationship with God is constantly under threat from personal weaknesses and inclinations to the seductive voices and gods of this world within and outside me. Thirdly, and most importantly, it is a public confession of the persistent and enduring character of God's love. His assurance through the prophet Jeremiah (31.3) is unalterably real: "I have loved you with an everlasting love". In no condition will he abandon the one he loves, even if humans can and do abandon the ones they love (Is. 49.15). There is no rock more solid than this assurance in the spiritual romance between a person and God, the father of our Lord Jesus Christ. The experience of this truth has been a source of deep joy and courage for me in moments of trials and doubts. Finally, this book expresses the gradual evolution of my deep love for the Church, the bride of Christ, and of the profound appreciation of the mission she has in the world. This mission of transforming the world with God's saving love in Jesus Christ is real and it has come to engage my entire being. This heightened awareness is the source of the passion I have for the formation of agents of evangelisation, especially the future priests. The things I have written in these pages did not come at once in my life. They are also not simply the result of mere intellectual research. They grew out of the desire to understand and make sense of my life and my vocation as a priest, and this desire grew over the years in the midst of trials and confusion.

From my seminary days, I dreaded living a life without passionate love. Though I did not understand it then, this was mainly the reason I asked my formators too many questions. I had a serious desire to serve God from the moment I was fascinated with the story of the call of Samuel at the age of eleven. My catechism teacher interpreted my fascination as a possible vocation to the priesthood. In fact, she encouraged me to take it seriously. I took then the name Samuel for my Confirmation, identifying myself with this prophet who, from a very tender age, was handed over to God. This profound attraction and desire never left me throughout the whole seminary training till today. However, during the seminary period, I suffered much confusion: on the one hand was this strong desire to serve God as a priest, and on the other hand, was the series of doubts and unanswered questions about the priesthood itself and my future life. My questions and search led me to some priests and books for direction. Along the line, I had moments of confusion and depression. The heavy academic formation in the seminary could only satisfy my intellectual curiosity but could not respond to the deep questions and yearnings of my heart. These doubts and confusion were lifted from me through what I eventually came to understand as an experience of God's immeasurable love. I cannot explain how it happened, but on the basis of that experience, everything became meaningful to me, and the decisive option was to follow the Lord Jesus, the Master who showed in his life what it means to live for others completely. I still relive the emotions I felt the day when I lay prostrate during my ordination as the litany of the saints was being sung. I felt myself totally consecrated to God whose love for me I could not doubt; it was this experienced love which has marked my existence, and made the relationship between me and Jesus the most important in my life. My whole life revolves around this relationship.

But life is not that rosy and constantly in this "romantic atmosphere" existing between me and God. Life questions and experiences, new information and increased knowledge brought in different kinds of doubts and problems. Personal needs and desires made their demands in the face of widespread values of the modern world informed by secular humanistic ideologies. This situation questioned my structure of meaning – the values Jesus proclaimed and lived, and the meaningfulness of the Catholic Church and priesthood – upon which I had constructed my life. Everything I believed in came crashing before the enormous doubts and questions emerging from within and outside me. The struggle was fierce and nearly drove me crazy. I needed some degree of insight and consolation. It was a most terrifying experience because the meaning of my life was at stake. Underneath this confusion and wavering of mind and heart, however, the love of God I experienced remained a reminder that I could not easily do away with. I realized in that experience that the major issue was not this sin or that sin, this weakness or that other one, but the fundamental position I take towards the whole of life. I wept many days and nights and could not reconcile contradictory strands of thoughts and emotions. I read a lot and reflected a lot in this condition. In his enduring love and gentleness, God who is love, gave me moments of insight into the unquestionable validity of the way I had been led. In the periods I had strayed in thoughts, deeds and words, the assurance of the permanence of his redeeming love remained an unshakable source of strength, courage, and joy.

As I turn fifteen in the priesthood, certain convictions have really come to take deep root in me. First, that God is love; that this love is unconditional and has become experientially meaningful. This love is enduring and redeeming. It holds the power to transform us in any condition we find ourselves. This love does not change no matter how bad and evil we become through our wrong choices and decisions. The personal response to this love cannot be understood and appreciated solely in moralistic terms; it is a response to love experienced. The transformation which God's love effects in a person takes hold of the whole person, leaving nothing untouched. It is in this reality that the pain of human weakness and the ambivalence of the human heart are felt so strongly. And here is my second conviction, expressed most beautifully by Francis LeBuffe in his commentary on Francis Thompson's classic poem *The Hound of Heaven*: "there is no greater pain than the anguish of the soul that is face to face with a great renunciation for God and finds not within itself sufficient generosity to make the surrender". This lack of generosity is not really an absence in an absolute sense marked by bad will or bad intention. Rather, it is largely a lack of spontaneity in giving oneself completely and totally to God. It makes the love adventure with God something tedious and sometimes frustrating because of one's inability to allow oneself to be completely taken over by God. My conviction therefore is: it is a painful experience not to be able to please the Lord as one would desire. This was also the greatest spiritual torture St. Augustine experienced as he wrote in his *Confessions:* "All doubt had been taken from me that there is indestructible substance from which comes all substance. My desire was not to be more certain of you but to be more stable in you. I was attracted by the way, the Saviour himself, but was still reluctant to go along its narrow paths". This reluctance is not really willed by Augustine; it is just that he desires to be completely taken over by the Lord whom he has come to know, but finds himself unable to do so. It is then that the grace of God broke the chains that bound him and freed Augustine to give his heart to God.

This second conviction leads to the third: God's call to be a priest is not because one is perfect or that one has understood everything, but because of His tremendous love. This conviction is the most humbling for me. In my weaknesses and confusion, his love remains constant, calling out to me in a manner that I am simply unable to run away from his presence – an experience beautifully expressed by Thompson in his poem, which resonates deeply with my experience.

These three strong convictions form the foundation upon which my life with the Lord is now restructured. It frees me from certain self-preoccupations and pretensions, and makes me a real person with flesh and blood, but marked with a deep sense of God's immeasurable love. It increases in me the attitude of gratitude, knowing everyday that all the good in me flows from His love. But I constantly struggle to love Him with all that I am and have. Though I do not succeed always, I trust in his infinite mercy and love. He knows I love Him deeply, though I suffer the pains of my inability to be totally his as my heart desires. This, in itself, is very unpleasant. Sometimes, it occurs to me that, perhaps, without this experience of incapacity, I would have become too arrogant and too confident. In the final analysis, "his ways are not our ways" (Is. 55.8).

I decided to make this writing public not only to mark my fifteenth year as a Catholic priest, but also to encourage my fellow priests to hold onto their faith in the face of the many trials we face today. This book is also a means of inviting each priest to search out the truth and make his own, the inner meaning of the priestly vocation in the Catholic Church. It is on this personal discovery and appropriation of the inner life of the priesthood that the deepest sense of fulfilment is experienced.

In the face of the many doubts regarding the Catholic priesthood today, every priest must make sense of his life and of the meaning and mission of the Church. I also write it for seminarians to provide them with some materials for personal reflection, to help them be more realistic in their vocational journey, and to know that experience of doubts and questions are not signs of lack of vocation. Rather, they constitute part of their efforts to discern their vocation and to strive towards internalizing genuine priestly identity. The tendency to spiritualize human situations, struggles and weaknesses should be resisted by a sharpened sense of realism and self-honesty. Each seminarian should make effort to confront his wrong and distorted motives for being a priest.

I thank God for the gift of priestly vocation and for his unceasing love for me. I offer Him the prayers which I made to Him on the day of my ordination, and which were on the souvenir of my priestly ordination. The prayer reads:

To love you Lord is my heart's desire
In all things to live for you
Leaving nothing to take me from you
Whose love is sweeter than honey

To obey you Lord is my sole desire
In every moment to choose you Lord
Leaving no seed of disobedience behind
To hinder my total embrace of you

To trust you Lord is my sole desire
Ever ready to follow you still
When earth's tempests sway me around
Making me faint in my faith in you

Hold me always my Lord and God
Dip me deep in your fount of grace
Enable me to cling onto you
Till you make me what you want

Acknowledgment

In a special way I thank my parents, my late Father, Reuben and my mother Veronica. Their openness to God and the love between them were great inspirations to me and the first reflection of God's love in my life. My brothers and sisters were of great assistance to my personal growth, but especially the love and care I experienced in the hand of my nurse-brother, Sir Ferdinand Okwuosa Okeke. I cannot fully express my indebtedness to him for his outstanding faith and courage in the great trials that assailed him in his life. I thank God for the gift of the spiritual directors who have helped me in various ways at different stages in my life, especially, in those periods of confusion and inner laceration: Frs. Anthony Asiegbu, Dom Collins Okafor, Stephen Njoku, Anthony Akabogu, John Fuellenbach SVD, and now Dominic Tataro SJ. I must include here, Sr. Marypat Garvin, who graciously accompanied me in my vocational growth experience. My encounter with her was a great experience of inner freedom. These are great persons in my life, though they may not be aware of it. With great affection I appreciate the significant impact of my professors at the Institute of Psychology in Rome, especially Fr. Barth Kiely SJ, from whom I learned a lot. The visible simplicity of their lives and deep commitment to God and humanity spoke deeply to my heart. The generosity of many people has been a concrete experience of God's providential care. I remember with gratitude Ron Brosofske and his family. Others are Wanda Edie, Bill and Maryann Holloway, Bill and Jan Roland, Bill and Margaret Terrien, Matthew and Carol Fett, Aline Irvin, and many others. I also appreciate the wonderful fraternal spirit existing among us, the formators at Pope John Paul II Major Seminary. It is an experience that enables us to enjoy the gift of each other, and to serve our beloved seminarians. The great openness of my seminarians towards me especially in sharing their doubts and hesitations is a great source of inspiration and admiration for me. I thank them for that. I am indebted to my friend, Fr. Innocent Nwafor, who read this work in its initial draft and made invaluable suggestions. I thank others who went through it: Frs. Christian Amogu, Cyril Udebunu, Victor Onwukeme, and Dr. Euchay Onyeizugbo. Your professional insights and constructive criticisms improved the quality and organization of the work. I remain grateful. Fr. Lawrence Nwankwor is my bosom friend whose encouragement and insights have always been great sources of confidence and hope. I have shared a lot with him, and I remain grateful. I deeply appreciate the fidelity and openness I enjoyed from priest-friends especially Frs. Ifunanya Aneke, Douglas Bignall, Chike Chukwuma, and Tony

Umeh. The final draft of this work was completed in the rectory of St. Benedict's Church, Waterford, Michigan. I thank the Pastor, Fr. Tom Kuehnemund, for providing me with the good environment I needed for the writing. The friendly discussions we had gave me important insights and motivated me more to continue on the journey of personal maturity. I remain grateful to him for our cherished friendship. To Rosecolette Ilechukwu who was the first to remind me that the fifteen years in the priesthood should be celebrated, I say a big thank you. And to all others who have made significant impact in my life and whose name I cannot mention here, I remain forever grateful.

Fr. Cornelius Uchenna Okeke
February 2, 2008
Feast of the Presentation of Our Lord

Introduction

No human being can survive a meaningless existence. Our life must make sense. This is the fundamental ache of every human being. When life makes sense, there is motivation, joy and sense of direction and general contentment. When life lacks sense, human beings lose the taste of living. This condition can drive some persons into different forms of pathologies. For some, the experience of lack of fulfilment is an occasion to wake up to the challenges of a more meaningful and fulfilled human existence.

Every Catholic priest faces the question of whether his life makes sense or not. This question comes in various ways and must be faced head on. For some, this question comes in the form of feelings of emptiness, and for others, it comes as a feeling of life slipping through the fingers. Yet, for some others, it manifests itself in a persistent feeling that life is better elsewhere. Fortunately, some are aware of the existential significance of the emptiness they feel in their lives. But there are many others who are unable to listen to themselves and embark on the journey of questioning and listening to themselves. This later group tends to externalize the problem in such a manner that their situation remains untouched.

Yet, the choice of externalization does not bring peace and contentment. To experience fulfilment as a Catholic priest, one needs to question oneself constantly as to the meaning of the priesthood and make it an integral aspect of one's self-definition.

The Catholic priesthood is a priceless gift of God to the Church, and for those of us called by God to it, we should consider ourselves trusted in a special way by God; trusted, not because of our goodness or holiness, but because of God's love and mercy. I consider this the starting point of priestly vocation. Whenever we priests become aware that God calls us in spite of ourselves, draws us closely to His heart, and entrusts us with the task of serving His people, we become overwhelmed with joy. The joy is a consequence of being loved in an unconditional way. God's love is not conditional as human love. When a priest realizes that he is so much loved to the point of being trusted to be given a responsibility, it is a pleasant experience that goes down to the depth of his being. The fact that every priest is called in spite of himself makes the priestly vocation a humbling one. No priest is chosen because he is the best among humans. We know from both church history and our experiences that priests are not the holiest of Christians; like the rest of Christians, we make effort to respond to the grace of God in our lives.

One becomes a priest because God has willed to call him through the Church. Our great fathers in faith are aware of this: Abraham was not called because he was better than Lot. There was no reason why God chose the people of Israel except that he loved them. It beats the judgment of common sense why Jacob should be chosen instead of Esau; nor does it make sense why Joseph was preferred to his other brothers. In the New Testament, Paul, a man consumed by his love for Jesus and for the Church, did not see any reason for being chosen for the missions in spite of his sinfulness. These are meant to show that every form of clerical arrogance, highhandedness or narcissistic sense of entitlement is anything but Christian and priestly. Every priest faces the challenge of relating to this starting point of priestly vocation and making it his own personal starting point.

The consciousness of being chosen by God to be a priest brings joy to every priest, as well as the desire and readiness to respond generously to this call. The fundamental response is opening one's heart to commit oneself to this call and its demands. No commitment is cost-free, otherwise it would not be commitment. The priesthood, like marriage, has its costs. Hence, it is not a privileged place of honour in a secular sense, and should not be taken to be so. For this reason, it is necessary to understand the set-apartness of priests: it does not mean that priests are more sacred, holy, privileged, exalted and unreachable or unlike the rest of Christians. This thinking usually leads to rugged clericalism, which does not have any grounding in experience. Rather, I see the set-apartness of the priest in the context of relationship: a married man is to a reasonable degree set apart for his wife, so that in a certain ontological sense he belongs wholly and entirely to his wife in the marital relationship. In a similar manner, a priest is one who has been *wooed* by God's love through the Church, and has, therefore, been *chosen* and set apart by the same God to serve Him and His people in the Church. This *choice* sets the priest apart as belonging to God and to the Church. But the priest also accepts this singular love of God and responds to this divine invitation. The determinant of set-apartness, therefore, is the love of God and service of His people which have so filled a person's heart that he decides to opt for the priesthood.

But the priesthood poses serious challenges. It expresses the affirmation of God's trust in us priests which is the foundation of our experience of meaning and fulfilment. But it could constitute a dangerous path for those who accept the trust, as well as for the Church and the world. Under the weight of human weaknesses and the liabilities of our different personalities, some of us priests fail to find meaning in their vocation. Trapped in their experience of meaninglessness, they begin to cast shadow instead of light, discourage, torment and cause harm to themselves and to other people.

The basic fact is that no human being is completely present to himself or herself. Sometimes we live in accordance with our vocation in life, and at another time we forget it completely and follow other conflicting inclinations. Occasionally, we may be overtaken by both conscious and unconscious powers which reduce our freedom to make the right choices that correspond to genuine Christian values we are called to embody. When these conscious and unconscious powers overtake any man or woman in any vocation, the individual may wreak havoc on himself and others: a doctor may break all the rules of his profession and take undue advantage of the patients; an accountant may falsify the accounts of the company he works for in order to enrich himself, which may lead to bankruptcy and loss of jobs; a pharmacist may lie about the components of a medication to make more money, even if it means endangering the health of others; a judge may make a decision against truth and justice to serve his own interest or that of his friends and so thwarts the process of justice; a policeman may use his training and equipment for criminal purposes; a lecturer may use his authority to intimidate students and extort money or pleasure from them; and a priest may use his position to obtain power, sexual gratification, or enrichment for himself. The variations are endless.

The possibility of these problems is always present in human nature, but the way and manner they are expressed depends on the personality of each person and the central values that guide him or her. Priests who are reasonably mature in their personalities tend to know and manage better the challenges of the priesthood than those who are immature. But maturity itself is not a point of arrival, as a process of continual inner work and self-knowledge in the light of what God is doing in each of us. Maturing priests are more aware of their psychological liabilities and the difficulties they generate in their lives. Psychologically immature priests have many unresolved developmental hang-ups that make the challenges of the priesthood very burdensome. The more embedded the immaturity, the greater the possibility that the shadow side of their personality will be out of control and exercise great influence in their lives. This leads to more cases of pathological liars; priests who are dupes; priests who exploit vulnerable persons without feeling any guilt; priests who are sexual predators; priests who wield power in their hands for domination, intimidation, and destruction of lives.

Living as a priest, like life itself, is an art and a challenge. As an art, its inner meaning is known through experience and deep reflection, and this demands the complete involvement of the whole being of the person called, both the conscious and the unconscious dimensions. As a challenge, priestly life asks for a continuous process of growth in one's humanity and vocation. But the starting point of the priestly life is a thorough understanding of what ordained ministry in the church means side by side with the relationship between the person and God. That is to say, the priest should know his identity in the Church and in the world. This provides him with an articulation of who he is and who he is called to be in the Church, which engages his whole life. Secondly, these ideals should find their way to his heart so that they can exercise an overriding influence in his thinking, sentiments, choices and decisions. The ideals of the priestly vocation, however, begin their journey in the heart of a priest through the experience of God's unconditional love which flows out as a sincere love for the Church. This is the manner in which vocation to the priesthood offers itself to be lived creatively, so that every priest embodies a uniqueness that expresses the authenticity of the priestly life and the uniqueness of the individual.

This small book is an attempt to provide, in a highly condensed manner, the various dimensions of the journey to a joyful and fulfilled life as a Catholic priest. It has three chapters, which I arranged in a very practical sequence. This arrangement was inspired by what I think good business people do to make progress in their business. Every good businessman will first of all be clear on what kind of business he wants in order to avoid serious confusion. Clarity regarding what he wants to do enables him to focus his energy and thinking on how to manage the amount of money he has. This is what I have tried to do in chapter one, where I present, in a general way, the identity of ordained priesthood. This theoretical clarification is very necessary for the priest because it saves him from certain cognitive confusion that could impact negatively on his life. From the Church's teaching, I try to sift out the essential elements that constitute the identity of a priest, drawing also from sociological and psychological studies.

When a businessman is clear as to what he wants to do, he is faced with how he has to go about it. This involves certain rules he has to abide by and certain moves he has to make. For instance, he cannot simply want to make a lot of profit without making sure he manages his capital well. This entails making proportionate expenses, taking the pains to get goods at a much cheaper rate and to have access to many customers. These constitute the dynamism of the business. A lot of sacrifices are involved. The gospel counsels constitute the dynamism of the priestly life because they express the radical nature of the priest's life, which derives from the vision of life inaugurated by Jesus Christ. In chapter two, I present the essence of this vision and how it is incarnated in these counsels, and how these counsels affect our spiritual and human development as priests. In presenting the content of this chapter, I draw heavily from the documents of the Church, biblical and psychological studies.

From time to time a businessman must evaluate his business to see if he is making progress or not. This evaluation is necessary for him to know which areas to improve and what changes to make. In general, he has to know if his business is growing and whether he is using all the resources at his disposal. Most importantly, he has to attune himself to the economic changes in society to assess the survival possibility of his business. If he does not do this from time to time, he may wake up one day and find his business crumbling to his surprise. In human living, the key factor that serves as a kind of thermometer in measuring the extent one is making progress or not is the level of satisfaction and/or dissatisfaction. But because human living is more complex than a business enterprise, the assessment demands deeper understanding and self-honesty. In chapter three, I present a kind of framework for evaluating our level of satisfaction and dissatisfaction as priests. This chapter is meant to enable priests be aware of how they feel generally about their lives as priests, and it invites them to look out for some clues as to what could be the source of their feelings of satisfaction or dissatisfaction in their vocation.

This arrangement is purposely adopted to help priests have a clear framework for self-evaluation. But it is also hoped to be useful for formators of future priests in clarifying the objectives of their formative interventions on their seminarians. From this, they could come up with certain practical modalities that will guide their evaluation of candidates.

Chapter One

Know Your Identity as a Catholic Priest

If you do not know where you are going you may not know how to get there. In the same manner, if you are not quite sure who you are, you may suffer different kinds of confusion. A clear sense of one's identity sets the ground for appropriate choices and decisions, gives direction to one's actions, and helps in organizing a person's thoughts and actions.

Basis for a Renewed Quest for Authentic Priestly Identity

Almost all over the Catholic world today, the question of priestly identity is discussed from different perspectives, such as theology, sociology, psychology, and history. Basic to the debates and the discussions is the issue of defining the nature and mission of the ordained priesthood in the Church, especially as the laity gets more involved everyday in the affairs of the Church since the Second Vatican Council. Even many decades after the Council, some priests still feel that the boundary between the ordained or ministerial priesthood and the common priesthood of the whole people of God remains blurred. To clarify the matter, two Synods of Bishops were held in 1967 and in 1990: the former dwelt on the meaning and place of the ministerial priest in the Church and the later dwelt on the formation of priests in the circumstances of today.

In different parts of Africa and Latin America, the involvement of the laity in the administration of the Church's affairs is not yet as pronounced as it is in the industrialized parts of Europe and North America. The Church remains largely the "father's Church" so that the clergy makes most of the decisions and defines responsibilities. But this does not imply that the problem of priestly identity is absent in these places. The problem of priestly identity in Africa, for example, is deeply rooted in the challenges posed by certain cultural values. For instance, some Catholic priests have become more or less fortune tellers and diviners, in the model of priests of the African Traditional Religion. Most of the time, their lifestyle does not even express the high moral and religious attitudes of the priests of African Traditional Religion. It becomes a kind of selective identification with the popular and financially profitable aspects of the traditional religion. It is often not clear to these priests what they are, whether Catholic priests or priests of the traditional religion. In the communitarian structure of the African cultures, some priests are not sure of where they belong in the social fabric.

There has been a variety of resolutions of this concrete dilemma ranging from extreme compromises to realistic appropriation of one's place in the African community[1]. In some parts of Africa, some priests have combined marriage and the priesthood and have eventually left the Catholic Church to join other Churches with their wives. These problems are not unrelated to the question of priestly identity and how priests come to realize it in their lives.

The Question of Identity: the Objective and Subjective Sides

The word identity denotes "the quality or condition of being a specified person or thing"[2]. The emphasis is on specification by means of which a thing or a person is differentiated from an-*other*, according to objective properties and characteristics. But there is the subjective side of identity, which directly expresses a person's experience of himself as this particular person. Identity understood in this subjective sense designates "a person's essential, continuous self, the internal, subjective concept of oneself as an individual"[3]; it is a person's "inner conviction, held as a whole or in relation to particular functions or roles, ... a stable awareness of who one is and where one is going, ..."[4]. Thus, there are two sides to identity: the objective and the subjective, and both are expressed in the life and personal consciousness of the individual.

It is necessary to understand the objective nature of priestly identity because there cannot be any real basis either for the formation of priests or the evaluation of our personal lives as priests, if the enduring elements that constitute the nature and mission of the ordained priesthood within the Church are not clear to both the formators and every one of us priests. As C.B. Daly observes, the greatest difficulty in the formation of priests today is that of differentiating between the permanent truths and values regarding the priesthood, and the contingent and time-conditioned disciplines and cultures. To be able to make such a distinction, it is important "to be clear about what is permanent and unchanging truth of faith in respect of the nature of Catholic priesthood itself"[5]. This is the surest guide for dealing with problems related to priestly identity, the formation of priests, and pastoral planning[6]. Formation and vocational growth are the processes through which individual priests make their own (subjective) the objective identity of the priesthood.

I shall draw out the teaching of the Church concerning priestly identity from the documents of the Second Vatican Council and from post-conciliar documents. This choice is made because my intention is not to present a detailed theology of the priesthood. Trained theologians can do that better than myself. My concern is simply to sift out the essential elements that characterise the ordained priesthood. For this limited purpose, I am not directly concerned with the history of the priesthood, or with the controversies surrounding the priesthood today. Again, there are countless books on these topics. In other words, authentic priestly formation aims at making the objective priestly identity become subjective or personal to each priest. The starting point of that process is a clear understanding of the objective side of priestly identity.

The Ordained Priesthood in the Church

Ministerial Priesthood within an Ecclesiology of Communion

Conciliar and Post-Conciliar teachings on the ordained priesthood usually move from the primordial priesthood of Christ, through the priesthood of all the faithful to the ministerial priesthood[7]. This method is in consonance with the ecclesiology of the Second Vatican Council, which understands the Church as primarily a *mystery*[8] of *communion*[9] with a *mission*[10]. The Church's nature as mystery is rooted in the incarnate Son of God who is at once truly God and truly man. This means that, "*the Church is a divine, transcendent, and salvific reality which is visibly present among men*"[11]. Her profound nature as *communion* is rooted in the self-giving love between the Three

5

Persons of the Holy Trinity. God, one in substance but three in persons, desires to bring all men and women to salvation so that they can share in this Trinitarian communion. This is the Trinitarian mission. Yet, in the bosom of the Trinity, each of the Three Persons has a specific mission within this one Trinitarian mission.

The heart of this conciliar ecclesiology is communion, which derives from and is rooted in the Blessed Trinity. This communion emphasizes the equality and distinctness of the three Persons of the Trinity. The equality between and the distinct personal identity of the Father, the Son, and the Holy Spirit are mirrored in the organic nature of the Church in which all members have different missions[12]. Thus, the Church is likened to an organic body with different parts, each having a different mission, but each part is also in relationship for the service of unity of the whole body. The distinct nature and mission of the ministerial priesthood is to be understood within this ecclesiology of communion[13].

The Lord Jesus has constituted the Church. He made all the baptized into a holy priesthood by giving them "a share in the anointing of the Spirit with which he was anointed"[14]. Sharing in the one priesthood of Christ, all the baptised can therefore offer spiritual sacrifices to God through Jesus Christ by proclaiming in and through their lives that they have been called out of darkness into the light of

Christ[15]. Every member of the Church shares in the priesthood and mission of the Church.

The Christocentric Element in the Identify of Ministerial Priests

Distinct from but related to the common priesthood is the ministerial priesthood. The Lord Jesus himself deemed it necessary to choose certain men as his ministers to exercise "the priestly office publicly on behalf of men and women in the name of Christ"[16]. "Called like the rest of those who have been baptised to become a true image of Christ (cf. Rom 8:29), the priest, like the Apostles, shares besides in a special way companionship with Christ and his mission as the Supreme Pastor"[17].

Therefore, the identity of the priest is rooted in his particular relationship with Christ. His election and consecration, by the power of ordination, configures him to Christ[18]. He is a "sacramental representation of Christ"[19], a living instrument of Christ the eternal priest[20]. In his ministry, the priest does not act in his own name; he acts *in persona Christi*,[21] representing Christ who acts through him with the power of the Holy Spirit. But if he acts *in persona Christi*, he also acts *in persona ecclesia* because he represents the People of God, the Church, to which he is united in Spirit[22]. Priests act *in persona ecclesiae* "not in the sense that they operate in place of the Church or that their ministry is delegated to them by the community, but in the sense that they should act as responsible signs and instruments in which and through which the Church effectively makes herself present and transmits the fruits of salvation"[23]. It is the identification with Christ which makes all priestly ministry fruitful[24]. The pastoral activities of the priest may therefore not be dissociated from his identification with Christ, which is the heart of his spiritual life.

The Threefold Functions of Priests

Election and consecration is for mission. Priests are chosen from among the faithful to further the work or mission of Christ, entrusted to the Apostles by Christ himself. They are chosen from among the people of God "not that they may be made distant from this people or from any man, but that they be totally dedicated to the work for which the Lord has raised them up"[25]. This work is the work of Christ entrusted to the apostles to be carried out under the power of the Holy Spirit and directed toward the Church[26]. The Church understands this work as exercised in the three functions of teaching, sanctifying and leading the Christian community. In carrying out these functions, the priest makes Jesus Christ and his work present in the community of the faithful and in the world. The post-synodal document, *Ultimis Temporibus*, states: "By effectively proclaiming the Gospel, by gathering together and leading the community, by remitting sins, and especially by celebrating the Eucharist, it makes Christ, the head of the community, present in the exercise of his work of redeeming mankind and glorifying God perfectly"[27]. The bishops as the direct successors of the apostles fully share in these functions of Christ while the priests, as the collaborators of the bishops, share in these functions at a subordinate level[28]. Let us explore in some depth the three functions outlined above.

The Ministry of Teaching

The priest proclaims the mystery of Christ in words and by the example of his life. Through his proclamation and teaching, he continuously invites men and women to deeper knowledge of and conversion to the truth of Jesus Christ which protects the people of God from the ravenous wolves of contemporary false and deceptive teachings[29]. The priest does not speak on his own authority but on the authority of Christ who called him and sent him through the Church. This implies that he can only teach the wisdom of Christ and not his own wisdom (II Cor. 4:5)[30]. Because this preaching is authoritatively carried out in the name of Christ, it "signifies a being 'with Christ', [and] in Christ it becomes redemptively efficacious"[31]. This should not be difficult to understand. The Igbo people have a proverb which says that *he who is close to a person knows the actual smell of the person's mouth.* In other words, the one who knows an-*other* in and out can speak authoritatively about that person. This knowledge is far deeper than an intellectual knowledge. It is a knowledge that is generally obtained through a bond of love existing between two persons. No matter how a CEO of a company is known in the media and by colleagues and business associates, the knowledge his beloved wife has of him is much deeper, more personal, and more authoritative because it is more encompassing. She knows him in his capacity as a business executive, but also as a sweetheart. This clearly brings out the importance of the deep relationship that needs to exist between the priest and Jesus Christ. It is a relationship that should be significantly personal. It is from this personal relationship that a priest proclaims the *Jesus Christ* that he knows.

The Ministry of Sanctification

The proclamation of the Word is directed to the full sacramental life of the Christian and of the Church. Through the sacraments the priest sanctifies himself and the people of God. Especially in the Eucharist, the pasch of Christ, the priest presents his own offering of himself and that of all the faithful, united with the supreme offering of Christ himself, to God the Father in the name of the Church. "Thus the Eucharist only makes plain, in symbolic and sacramental efficacy, the goal towards which the whole apostolic ministry of the priest is directed: preaching the faith and pastoral care as well as administration of the sacraments"[32].

The Ministry of Leadership

The ordained priesthood differs essentially from the priesthood of the whole Church[33]: it exists *for the sake of* the universal priesthood[34], for the service it renders to the common priesthood. Jesus did not choose the apostles to give them places of honour; he chose them *to be with Him* and *to minister* to the people. Thus the leadership of the ministerial priesthood is to serve the people of God, enabling the "unfolding of the baptismal graces of all the Christians"[35]. The priestly office is ministerial precisely because it is fundamentally a service in love[36]. The headship of the priest is modelled after the headship of Christ, which is "a headship of love, a headship of self-giving, a headship of self-sacrifice, a headship of service.... Any day on which ministerial priesthood is perceived as domination or monopoly is a day on which what should be light has been turned into darkness"[37].

Thus the priest, rooted in his relationship with Christ, carries out the leadership of service through the exercise of the three functions Christ entrusted to the apostles, and in so doing builds the Church at both the local and universal levels. Therefore, the identity of the priest derives from these two dimensions of the priesthood: identification with Christ and service of the Church[38]. Seminarians, therefore, who are in training for the priesthood should prepare themselves by growing towards greater intimacy with Christ in order to exercise effectively the ministry of the word, the ministry of worship and sanctification, and the ministry of shepherding God's flock[39].

What stands out clearly in the conciliar and post-conciliar teachings explored above is that the whole theology and spirituality of the ordained ministry in the Church are centered on the person of Jesus Christ. It is true that all Christians, and this includes the priests, have a special relationship to Christ by virtue of their baptism and participation in the life of the Church. By this very fact, everyone is called to holiness of life. But, having publicly accepted to serve God and His church as a priest, "the ordained minister has committed himself to be a public holy person in the holy Church"[40]. And this means "a configuration with Christ in his very mission and ministry, which includes the preaching, sanctifying and teaching mission and ministry"[41]. This is the theological basis of priestly life and ministry, and it is that which differentiates a priest from other members of Christ's faithful.

Having sketched out the identity of the ordained ministry in the Church, I will now go on to specify further the dimensions of its inner life, and the implications it has in our concrete life as priests.

The sketch above gives us the general structure of the priestly vocation. In the next section, I shall focus on identifying the contents of this structure drawing from the studies in the sociology and psychology of vocation.

The Essential Elements of Priestly Identity

The nature and mission of our lives as the ordained ministers in the Church and in the world implies a particular manner of being and living, intrinsically bound to the manner of being and living of Christ. Our whole being as priests should be marked by our identification with Jesus Christ. Our lives will have to reflect the *being of Christ* for "it is impossible to separate the *being* of the priest from the *being* of Christ, the *life* of the priest from the *life* of Christ"[42]. The Decree on the Ministry and Life of Priests, *Presbyterorum Ordinis*, of the Second Vatican Council, in Chapter III sets forth three elements that constitute the essence of this specific mode of *being* and *living* of the priest. The three elements are first, identification with Christ, which is effected by our election and consecration; second, our mission, which is tied to the mission of Christ; and third, the radical nature of our life, which is expressed in living the evangelical counsels. In his post-synodal apostolic exhortation, *Pastores Dabo Vobis*, John Paul II focuses upon these three elements and builds the spiritual life of the priest upon them[43]. The first element speaks of the *being* of the priest (*esse*); the second speaks of the *doing* of the priest (*agere*); and the third speaks of the *radical life of the gospel* that animates both the being and the doing of the priest. These three elements express the contents of the priestly identity, i.e., the values of the priesthood. I shall focus on the first and second elements in this chapter since they deal with the being and doing of the priest. In the second chapter, I shall examine the third element which constitutes the dynamism of the priestly vocation.

The Being of a Priest: Priestly Life is a Vocation

God is the one who calls the priest and consecrates him to Himself. Like the Apostles, the priest is *to be with Jesus* first, in order to be sent out to preach. Although "being with Jesus" and "being sent forth" are inseparable, the former precedes the latter. As Avery Dulles elaborates: "they must be with Jesus for the sake of their own conversion, which involves learning what he has to teach, acquiring his mentality, his style of existence and thinking; but they must also go forth so as to meet the spiritual needs of others, wherever the demands of the Church's mission require"[44]. This is true of us priests as it was for the Apostles. By consecrating us to Himself, God lays claim to the totality of our existence as His close allies and living instruments. Wulf notes that "by irrevocably calling a man to such a ministry, God sets him apart, lays his hand upon him, claims him for himself and for his work, so that the one who is called and commissioned has to put himself, as an instrument, at God's (Christ's) disposal. In this sense he is consecrated to God"[45].

Consecration and mission are intrinsically related in a dynamic manner. Thus the claim God makes upon us by virtue of our vocation and consecration is both the foundation and the source of the power we exercise in our mission. By calling and consecrating the priest to himself, God endows him with "spiritual powers" to carry out the mission to be entrusted to him[46]. Priestly vocation and consecration demands from us priests first and foremost a lively and unbroken relationship with Jesus Christ, the head and the shepherd[47]. Laghi expresses this well: "before his service to the community, what qualifies the priest is his unique communion with Christ, the new relationship which is established between Christ and the priest. I believe it is necessary that priests should recover the primacy of love for and contemplation of Christ, which gives their priesthood its most profound meaning"[48]. The basic reason is that of ourselves we, like the Apostles, can do nothing without Jesus Christ (Jn.15:5). In his *Called to Communion,* Cardinal Ratzinger, now Pope Benedict XVI, powerfully observes that "nothing that makes up the activity of the apostles is the product of their own capabilities. But it is precisely in having 'nothing' to call their own that their communion with Jesus consists, since Jesus is also entirely from the Father, has being only through him and in him and would not exist at all if he were not a continual coming forth from and self-return to the Father. Having 'nothing' of their own draws the apostles into communion of mission with Christ. This service, in which we are made the entire property of another, this giving of what does not come from us, is called sacrament in the language of the Church"[49]. Our being as priests flows back and forth in our communion with the being and mission of Jesus Christ.

This intimate relationship with Jesus Christ renders us more responsive to the promptings of the Holy Spirit. Although the Church believes that our weaknesses do not impede the action of grace in our ministry, she maintains, however, that "God ordinarily prefers to show his wonders through those who are more responsive to the impulse and guidance of the Holy Spirit and who, because of their intimate union with Christ and their holiness of life, are able to say with St. Paul: 'It is no longer I who live, but Christ who lives in me'"[50]. This is not to say that we are perfect men, but that we need to cultivate closeness with Jesus for greater conversion of our hearts to that of Jesus.

Priesthood is not a Career in a Narrow Sense

All this is meant to establish the true meaning of the ordained ministry in the Church: it is a religious vocation and, therefore, is different from a career or a profession or an occupation. A career is commonly understood as basically a profession or specialization a person enters into mostly because it is lucrative. Career promises power, status, and financial security, but does not necessarily bring peace and fulfilment. In this sense, a career could be a person's job; it may not necessarily express a person's passion. Henri Nouwen is one of the greatest spiritual writers in the recent times. He reached the height of his teaching career at Harvard University. But "after twenty years in the academic world as a teacher of pastoral psychology, pastoral theology, and Christian spirituality, I began to experience a deep inner threat. Everyone was saying that I was doing really well, but something inside was telling me that my success was putting my soul in danger".[51] The oppression he felt inside was that of his vocation as a priest. He was losing the "soul" of his life, his priestly vocation to a successful career. His teaching career gave him popularity, power, status, and even money. He was honest with himself. He prayed and listened to the Spirit of God. Then came the important choice in his life: "So I moved from Harvard to L'Arche, from the best and the brightest, wanting to rule the world, to men and women who had few or no words and were considered, at best, marginal to the needs of our society".[52] The handicapped people at L'Arche helped him to recover himself and his vocation. A great paradox indeed! The same was true with

James Hollis, one of the world's renowned Jungian psychologists. After many years of teaching and research career, he finally found his vocation in being a Jungian therapist. In fact, his book, *Finding Meaning in the Second Half of Life*, includes many examples of people who have to give up their career in search of their passion – their vocation. Toni Raiten-D'Antonio, the writer of the classical book *The Velveteen Principles*, studied theatre as her career. After her graduation, she worked for a public television station. Despite the financial security she had, she was miserable at her job. She suffered the pain of 'careerism' which smothered her passion and vocation. This happened until she picked up the courage to leave behind career and follow where her vocation was – to be a therapist. Today, she has blossomed. The development of the principles of being a real person in her seminal book is a result of the journey she went through to become real in her vocation. In a real sense, *our vocations call us to it*, but *we generally choose our career*. In a very broad sense, all vocations are from God because they express our identification with God's plan for us and for the world. That is why vocation generally brings fulfilment, peace, and joy in spite of all the sacrifices and pains involved. Over and above this, the Catholic priesthood is primarily a religious vocation and derives its sense and purpose in the Christian religion. Not to understand this can lead to some frustration and emptiness.

Vanoosting draws out four chief characteristics of every vocation in the Judeo-Christian tradition: first, a person is called *for a special purpose*; secondly, the person who is called has a special gift which "should not be confused with aptitude, skill or talent" [53]. Thirdly, vocation presupposes a *caller* which, in Judeo-Christian tradition, has a name – Yahweh, God, Jesus. Fourthly, acceptance of the vocation entails a *life of sacrifice, faith and often darkness*. The heart of these four characteristics is the relationship that exists between the caller and the one called, from which the one called learns the purpose of his vocation.

Priestly Vocation Transcends Career

It frequently happens that the priestly vocation is studied alongside secular professions. A relevant example is the study of Nigerian priests by J.B.C. Okorie using the psychological theories and constructs that are generally used for secular professions[54]. The basic aim of these studies is to analyse the motivational forces operative in a person's choice of career. Their general presupposition is that a vocational choice is an expression of one's self-concept[55]. Choosing a career based on the way a person sees himself implies that the chosen career will be the avenue for the person to exercise his potentialities and thereby achieve self-actualisation. If the expression of self-concept determines the choice of a career and this leads to the realisation of the self, then it implies that self-actualisation is the primary motivational force in the human being, and it consists in the realization of one's basic potentialities.

This anthropological presupposition is insufficient to explain or understand the vocation of the priest and the entire Christian vocation; it does not do justice to the inner reality of priestly vocation. The one called by God is not called to actualise himself merely by giving expression to his so-called basic potentialities[56]. He is called to expropriate, dispossess or transcend himself *because of* love of God and of humanity. And it is through this self-expropriation, self-dispossession, and self-transcendence in self-giving to God and to humanity that he realises himself fully as a human being[57]. Only he who loses himself can find himself (Mk. 8:35; Mt. 16: 24-25). This implies that "both self-transcendence and self-realisation are present in the Christian vocation. But the first is the cause of the second and the second is the effect, *not vice versa*, ..."[58].

The priesthood is not meant to be a career that advances one's social status. It should not be for the satisfaction of any human ambition or personal project[59] or even be taken as a human right to be demanded by, or conceded to everyone as long as he is a human being and a Christian[60]. Indeed, priestly ordination "is not about the development of one's own powers and gifts. It is not the appointment of a man as a functionary because he is especially good at it, or because it suits him, or simply because it strikes him as a good way to earn his bread; it is not a question of a job in which someone secures his own livelihood by his own abilities, perhaps in order to rise to something better"[61]. It is rather the "fruit of being chosen, it is the fruit of a specific vocation: '[Jesus] called his disciples, and chose from them twelve' (Lk. 6:13-16)"[62]. In this connection, Costello has been able to sift out from the reflections of the Fathers of the 8th Synod of Bishops on Priestly Formation three basic anthropological elements that characterise the priestly vocation and distinguish it from secular careers: "First, the priesthood is an internal grace offered by God to an individual for the service and mission of the Church. Second, the priesthood lays claim to the whole of the person's existence and in this respect cannot be understood as an occupation in the normal sense of the term. Third, the priesthood involves a new call to holiness of life not only in virtue of baptism …"[63].

The Danger of Taking the Priesthood merely as a Career

It is therefore an error to view the priesthood as a source of ego-enhancement, a project of self-fulfilment, a job, or an occupation. This understanding is very dangerous both to the priest and to the Church. First, a priest who sees his vocation as a job or a mere occupation or career can be tempted to detach his life from his ministry, so that while the gospel he preaches challenges his listeners, he does not subject himself to its influence. Secondly, taking the priesthood as an avenue to enhance one's ego can turn the priest into an egoistic monster who is guided by the principles of personal convenience and comfort. This is one of the dangers of the priesthood because it is one of the reasons why some priests exploit those entrusted to their care in various ways. But most importantly, living too long with this frame of mind usually makes the priest feel that something is missing in his life. A persistent feeling of this lack could lead to different forms of compensatory behaviours such as binge drinking, eating, smoking, sexual acting out and so on. Ordained ministry in the Church is a vocation, a gift of God's grace "not conferred for the honour or advantage of the recipient, but for the service of God and the Church; it is the object of a specific and totally gratuitous vocation: 'You did not choose me, no, I chose you; and I commissioned you...'"[64].

In summary, it is evident from this first element that priestly vocation is a vocation to serve God and others in total self-giving and to spend oneself for others. It is not a career in the narrow sense of the word. It should not be entered into for the primary purpose of expressing one's potentialities. It is not a means of achieving self-importance or simply a means of advancing one's social standing. It is a call to unite closely with Christ in service of

God and humanity. *Pastores Dabo Vobis* clearly states that priestly vocation "is a call, by the sacrament of holy orders received in the Church, to place oneself at the service of the People of God with a particular belonging and configuration to Jesus Christ and with the authority of acting 'in the name and in the person' of him who is head and shepherd of the Church"[65].

Priesthood: a Ministry that Requires Professionalism

The second element is our mission, which is to minister to the people of God entrusted to us. Ministry is not the same with discharging the duties of one's profession. The distinction between the two is subtle. Profession in the technical sense captures the reality of the priesthood to an extent. Priesthood is a profession in the sense of assenting to the full definition of what it means to be a priest.

Understanding Priestly Ministry and Professions

Priestly ministry is sometimes viewed and studied as a profession like the medical, legal and other such professions. Priests in some countries are accorded the status of professionals and are studied as such[66]. This notwithstanding, there is unity in difference between a profession and a ministry. Some writers emphasise the unity aspect while others emphasise the difference. But a balanced view, in my opinion, has to see the convergence between both without eliminating the differences. Some professions can be carried out as ministries while ministries necessarily require professionalism which does not exhaust the requirements. Professional teachers, for instance, make sure they teach what they are supposed to teach the students, not more, not less. But when a teacher begins to see his teaching as a vocation and ministry and not simply as a profession, he not only teaches what he is supposed to teach, but becomes a source of life and encouragement to the students; even the style of teaching changes. His teaching goes beyond the subject he teaches; he becomes a source of hope and inspiration to the students; his teaching relates to the meaning of life, far beyond the restricted confines of his subject. The students easily realize that he does not merely perform his duty as a teacher of, say, mathematics; he is larger than that. Such teachers have become, to some extent, ministers to the students. In other words, they not only teach; they serve their students. It is this service that is the essence of ministry. But the ministry of the priest is founded on the spiritual goods given to human beings by God through Jesus Christ, in the Holy Spirit. The priest serves the people of God the saving values of the Gospel. Through his ministry, the people of God experience deeper meaning of life, transformation of their lives and the human society, and look forward to the promised beatific vision of God in the world to come.

If some professionals like teachers grow to see their work as not simply a discharge of professional duty, how much more we, as priests, should avoid seeing our mission as mere duty to be performed. We are consecrated for a mission. The nature of our vocation as priests sets the context for understanding this mission: it is a ministry of service. The ministry primarily belongs to Jesus Christ, the head of the Church. We have been called, as sacramental representations of Jesus Christ, to continue His ministration in the Church and through the Church. Therefore, we may not take ourselves or be taken as functionaries, or mere professionals who simply carry out their duties. We do not just have the job of "managing" the Church[67]; ours is a vocation to lead the people of God with the authority of Jesus, that kind of authority that is expressed as service[68]. We are entrusted with a mission that is not our own.

For Gula, there is nothing wrong in maintaining that the priesthood is a profession and that priests should exercise the ministry as professionals. His argument is that, in the past, a profession was understood as "having a vocation". The word "professional" then carried the connotation of one who was motivated to dedicate himself to the service of the community. In this regard, Gula maintains that "the trademark of being a professional in the classical sense entailed the commitment to acquire expert knowledge and skills and to serve human needs with good moral character. Ideally, then, professionals are to reflect a high degree of congruence between what they publicly declare to be committed to and the way they carry out their tasks"[69]. Wilensky agrees with Gula noting that, traditionally, professionalism emphasises "autonomous expertise and the service ideal"[70]. But according to him, this traditional model was mostly limited to law and medicine[71]. As time went on, the desire to be professionalized increased and there emerged, as a result, mixed forms of control. Today, the understanding of professions has greatly shifted from this classical sense, as Gula acknowledges[72]. The way it is studied today sheds light on the evolution of the term and reveals the implications it would have for the priesthood, if it were to be taken like any secular profession.

In order to assess priestly ministry as a profession, there is need for a theoretical understanding of what a profession means. Some criteria have been identified to distinguish professions from other more general occupations[73]: namely, *structural* and *attitudinal* attributes. The structural attributes emphasise that professions are embedded in the social structure. This means that there are rules and regulations which guide the selection, admission, and training of the professionals and their operation in society as well as in the profession itself. The attitudinal attributes focus on the beliefs and values held by the professionals themselves[74].

Professions also maintain their autonomy. As a structural attribute, the autonomy of professions involves the efforts professionals make to exclude unqualified persons and legally safeguard the right of the members to practice a profession. As an attitudinal attribute, professional autonomy stresses the professional's competence in making certain judgements based on his expertise, which is recognised or questioned by other professionals[75]. Thus, professional status provides "role clarity, public recognition, enhanced social standing, personal competence and responsibility"[76].

Gannon takes issue with the professional model of priestly ministry. He argues that both the structural and attitudinal attributes of professions do not wholly apply to priestly ministry because the *context* and the *significance* of the priestly ministry are quite different from that of secular professions. The context and the significance of the priestly ministry "is the Church and *not*, as with other professions, *society-at-large*"[77]. The priest has no legitimacy or existence outside the Church and the Church's mission. He does not have the problem of gaining access to the Church as would happen in professions; his responsibility is to take up the mandate of the Church and carry out the mission attached to the role of the priest in the

Church[78]. The problem in applying the professional model to priestly ministry is therefore one of interpretation: since "priest" is primarily something one is and not merely something one does, it calls for an existential and not functional interpretation.

Costello supports the position of Gannon. He argues that it would be self-defeating to the individual priest and to ministry if ordained priesthood were taken like any secular profession. In the first instance, professionalism "embodies the values of competence and expertise in the performance of priestly tasks and functions..."[79] and tends to neglect the basic identification of the priestly life and mission with that of Christ. This identification of the priestly ministry with the ministry of Christ makes the priest's imitation of Jesus Christ the foundation and thrust of his life and ministry. In the second instance, a professional tends to put emphasis on the competence he demonstrates in his profession. For instance, a professional computer engineer working for a company brings his professional expertise to bear on the work he does. His duty is to make sure that he gives the professional services for which he is paid. He is not worried about the life of the customer and the customer is not interested in how he lives his life. He just performs his duty, and that is all.

Personal competence implies that one has to prove one's capability or mastery in one's profession. But this is not the central issue in priestly ministry, though it should not be absent. In professions, the emphasis is on the professional's personal effort, which has gained him the reward of being admitted into the profession. The norms of measurement are those of demonstrated performance and competence. The priesthood, on the other hand, is a spiritual calling; the norms of performance and competitiveness are difficult to standardize in spiritual matters[80]. That is why *the goal of priestly formation is not simply to produce persons who have scientific competence and pastoral skill, but, principally, to foster in those persons "a 'mode of being' in communion with Christ and those qualities which characterised his dealings with others"[81], "a way of being in communion with the very sentiments and behaviour of Christ the good shepherd"[82].* The seminary, therefore, "is a school of life and not a job, a global experience of faith and of the Church and not merely a training in order to carry out a profession decently"[83]; it is not for men "looking for roles, titles, and uniforms to disguise identity, but men looking for holiness and God through which to express identity"[84].

Pastoral Charity: Ministering with Professional Care

Because priestly vocation is a call to love God and humanity, there is need for a personal relationship to exist between the priest and Jesus Christ who calls him. The pastoral charity of the priest expresses this personal and intimate relationship between him and Jesus Christ; it is the animating principle of the priest's being and mission[85]. In *Pastores Dabo Vobis,* John Paul II describes the essential element of the pastoral charity of the priest as "the *gift of self*, the *total gift of self* to the Church, following the example of Christ. Pastoral charity is the virtue by which we imitate Christ in his self-giving and service. It is not just what we do, but our gift of self, which manifests Christ's love for His flock. Pastoral charity determines our way of thinking and acting, our way of relating to people. It makes special demands on us"[86]. Pastoral charity is the heart of priestly ministry and Jesus is the model. It consists in the total gift of self for the sake of others; it depicts that "way of thinking and acting proper to Jesus Christ"[87], the head of the Church. Though He is the head of the Church, Jesus lived his pastoral charity as a servant. For Him, to be the head of the Church would mean to be the servant of the Church.

There are two central objectives of the pastoral charity of Christ, namely, the *salvation of men* and *the glory of God*. This twofold objective in the life and ministry of Jesus Christ reached its fullest expression in his death on the cross[88]. The supreme sacrifice of Christ is re-enacted sacramentally in the Eucharistic sacrifice. Therefore, our life as priests has two foci: "the pasch of Christ, from which all that he can effect as a priest flows, and the glory of the eschatological kingdom, which proclaims the glory of God"[89]. In other words, by our pastoral charity, we dedicate our whole life to the salvation of mankind as Christ himself did. In doing so, we promote the eschatological kingdom, which is the glory of God. Thus, priestly vocation is directed to the kingdom of God and is concretely expressed in gift of the self.

In concrete terms, this attitude of pastoral charity is shown in the qualities of the good shepherd[90], who is Jesus Christ himself. Like the good shepherd, we must pay special attention to the weak and the fallen[91], have compassion for the flock of Christ[92], gather and protect them, search out the lost, visit and comfort the sick and the dying, listen to the troubles and pains of the faithful as they experience life crises[93], and we should be ready to spend ourselves and be spent in whatever office is entrusted to us, "however lowly and poorly rewarded"[94]. All this is possible only to the extent we deepen our openness to the love that God has poured into our hearts in Jesus Christ, for "only in loving and serving Christ, the head and spouse, will charity become a source, criterion, measure and impetus for the priest's love and service to the Church, the body and spouse of Christ"[95].

Laghi sums up the spirituality of the pastoral charity of the priest in three components: the spirituality of the *spouse*, the spirituality of the *servant* and the spirituality of the *brother*. Pastoral charity as the spirituality of the *spouse* emphasises our total and undivided love for Christ and for his Church; the spirituality of the servant indicates that as priests, we come to serve, we act not in our own name but in the name of Christ; the spirituality of the brother sees the presbyterium as the primary community of faith in which we share our faith and experience with the brother priests[96]. These three aspects of the pastoral charity of the priest are meant to express the rootedness of the ordained priesthood in Christ and in the Church. That is why Rypar calls it the ascetic principle around which the priesthood revolves[97], and Danneels firmly believes that it is precisely because of this pastoral charity that the position of the priest is that of a shepherd and not a governor or an animator of the assembly of God[98].

Professionalism or competence is good in itself, and it is necessary that we experience ourselves as competent. Secondly, the church, as an organisation, also needs competent persons to take charge of its mission of evangelisation. As priests, we should be competent preachers of the word and teachers of doctrine; we should demonstrate mastery in the administration of the sacraments and the temporal goods of the church; we should be able to exude confidence in our lives and in the pastoral activities. We should lead the people entrusted into our hands with the professional care of the Good Shepherd.

The Problem of Efficient but Ineffective Ministry

Our competence or professionalism should express our whole life. To overemphasise mere competence in the priestly vocation could turn our ministries as priests into a matter of organisational skill and efficiency. However good competence may be in itself, over-emphasis of it may make priests struggle to be merely efficient in their apostolate; but they may not be effective. This is another danger. Apostolic efficiency "has to do with the *means* used to present the values of Christ", while apostolic effectiveness is "the visible manifestation and/or the social communication of the values of Christ"[99]. A priest may be a good communicator but his life is a scandal that scares people away from him and from the Church. Another priest may be a competent scholar who knows the details of the Church's teaching, but he has no time either for God or for the people. In certain parts of the Catholic world, it is widely noticed among the faithful that a priest may be good at fund-raising and construction of buildings or management of other infrastructure in a parish. This is a source of pride to the parishioners. But when the same faithful are in crises, they may seek out priests other than their parish priest. By this attitude, the faithful are saying that though their parish priest is *efficient* in building and constructing the structures of their parish, he is not *effective* enough to be approached with their personal, spiritual or family problems.

It is important that we are both efficient and effective. In certain aspects, the church witnesses a stunning lack of both efficiency and effectiveness among some of its priests such that there is a subculture of mediocrity and spiritual turpitude. For this reason, we have among us priests, boring preachers who are good at sending people to sleep during homilies. There are priests who celebrate the sacraments carelessly and mindlessly. Still, there are those who are lazy and unconcerned in their apostolate. Effectiveness should be able to include efficiency so that the priest can be a true leader of the faithful especially in the highly challenging circumstances of today.

In the apparent struggle between efficiency and effectiveness, efficiency seems often to win especially because of its relationship with public visibility. We all want to be seen, noticed, recognized, and to be popular. To the extent this desire is strong and not worked on, to that extent we are driven in search of it. Hence, a priest may be preoccupied with how he renders his homily not so much as to be affected in his life by what he preaches as to the kind of impression he leaves on the people. Another may be so worried about the structures for which he will be remembered in the parish when he leaves, that the whole pastoral ministry is reduced to this search for social significance. The more priestly tasks gain greater visibility and recognition, the greater the motivation.

There is a serious psychological risk for priests if too much emphasis is placed on personal competence or efficiency in priestly tasks and functions without a deepening of relationship with Jesus Christ, which entails the internalisation of His values and sentiments. The risk is that such emphasis tends to highlight more the role of the priest than the values of the priesthood. This condition does not lead automatically to the acquisition of priestly identity[100]; in the long run, it may leave in the life of the priest a feeling of being a performer without a clear understanding of his identity[101]. This is the reason why some priests could be professors in secular universities, journalists, principals of schools, great administrators with financial and social positions; yet, they still feel empty within themselves because what they are, may not be clear to them. They feel their life is meaningless, not fulfilled. This is a condition that can lead one to behaviours that may be destructive to self and others. These priests who are professionals in other fields tend to identify themselves more in those professions than in their basic vocation as priests. Anthony de Mello calls such priests hyphenated priests. He says of them: "we have priest-worker, the priest-scientist, the priest-artist. We have apostles who are concerned to take up some profession or other as a help to their apostolate. All very well, indeed, *provided they keep fully alive what is most characteristic of their vocation as apostles, the ability to communicate the Holy Spirit to others*"[102]. Their priesthood gives them public prestige but not deep satisfaction. So, they look for consolation in being hyphenated.

The problem is often over-identification with the role they occupy as priests[103]. Such over-identification with a role makes one's genuine identity extrinsic to the self, which is a psychological condition that deepens the vulnerability of the self to the extent that it may not easily withstand inevitable changes that touch the role[104]. Drennan observes that the "identity of the crisis" of the "crisis of priestly identity" is to be found in this over-identification with the roles or functions the priest performs. He traces the history of priestly identity from the Old Testament through the Priesthood of Christ and establishes the foundation of priestly identity in the profound relationship with God in which the priest lives totally for God. This identity remains even when roles or functions change. It is basic then that "priestly identity that is based on particular roles or functions is vulnerable to crisis when a change of role is required"[105].

In summary, ministerial priesthood is a religious vocation *to minister*, that is, to serve humanity after the mind of Christ. Pastoral charity is the inner principle of priestly ministry and not the doling out of sacraments and other priestly activities in an efficient but maybe ineffective way.

As a religious vocation it "engages the whole person, public and private, thus demanding a profound integration between personal and occupational identity"[106]. The assertion of A. Ukwuoma that, "the priesthood should be considered as a profession because there is human labour involved in what the priest accomplishes in his ministry to the parishioners"[107] is simplistic and confusing. He fails to see the Christian anthropology that underlies the priestly vocation. Even if we were to accept what he asserts, it is important to observe that it is not just human labour that qualifies one as a professional; there is more to being a professional than that. While the professional may detach his private life from his professional duty, as priests, we may not detach our ministerial activities from our private lives without incurring serious injury to our lives and to the Church's mission of evangelisation. If it does not seem to matter that the manager of a company, a professional, cheats on his wife and neglects his children provided it does not affect the productivity and maximum profit of the company, it matters a lot that we who render the service of the Church in preaching the Gospel should struggle constantly to validate our preaching with a life of witness[108]. That is ministry with professional care. We may not succeed all the time, but it is a demand our vocation makes on us because it is the primacy of our being as priests that gives direction and efficacy to our ministry. Thus one can conclude that the priesthood is a vocation and ministry whose minimum requirement is professionalism. It is not simply a profession in the narrow sense of that word.

Summary of the Elements of Priestly Identity

The key phrase that sums up the elements that constitute the heart of priestly identity is *gift of self*. Priestly existence is that in which the priest is called by God *to give himself* to God and to the people of God and *not take away* from the people. His is *a vocation* to be with Christ and to be sent on a mission. Thus, Christ in him and through him continues His mission in the world, continuously giving Himself to the world and creating unity among peoples, which is the heart of the new Kingdom of God. His mission is, therefore, *to minister* to the world with the same pastoral charity of Christ. A priest is not a mere professional who prides himself on having gained entrance into the profession and who, therefore, from time to time, should be rewarded with promotions to more prestigious positions if he consistently demonstrates his competence in tasks. His radicalism in living the Gospel shows that the priesthood is of a different order, the order of the spiritual, of discipleship, of self-transcendence in love of God and of His Kingdom. The motivation to live a priestly life is "teleological and axiological, that is, it aims at goals which are values, these being in the last analysis the objective and self-transcendent values revealed by Christ"[109]. Costello sums up the core values of the priestly vocation from the Second Vatican Council, the *Catechism of the Catholic Church* and from the *Pastores Dabo Vobis*. They are: "Union with Christ the priest, holiness of life, the evangelisation of humanity, proclamation of God's Word, sacramental celebration, pastoral charity, prayer on behalf of the Church, ecclesial service, eucharistic devotion, evangelical simplicity of life, fidelity to the gospel, celibacy for the sake of the kingdom of God, a total and permanent commitment"[110].

In this chapter I have tried to examine the two elements of the priestly identity, namely the being and doing of the priest. In the next chapter, I shall present the dynamic element of our lives as priests, which is embodied in the vision of God's Kingdom, and expressed in the Gospel Counsels.

Chapter Two

The Vision of Life Underlying Priestly Life

It is important to realize that priestly vocation is essentially a spiritual calling. I have to keep this truth constantly before me in all circumstances. If I see myself outside this framework, my life loses direction. Though the Church teaches this, I believe that every priest must come to a personal realization of the truth of this teaching. It is in this framework that the vision of life that underlies priestly vocation should be intensely reflected upon and appropriated. Every priest must appreciate this Christian vision of life and make it his own. It is a significant step to the experience of fulfilment in one's vocation.

The Reign of God's Kingdom as Central to the Christian Vision of Life

Christian life entails a vision of life clearly represented and expressed in the person of Jesus of Nazareth. That new vision is condensed in the Sermon on the Mount (Mt. 5), and it is a total reversal of the prevailing world order in which money, power, control, domination, superiority, celebrity status, and the likes are promoted with so much violence and rivalry[1]. The interests and conveniences of the self, of one's family, group, of one's ethnic or national belonging often determine relationships, choices and decisions. Hence in this world the leaders lord it over those they lead (Mt. 20.24-25), and people engage in unhealthy competition for recognition and places of honour (Mt. 18.1-4; 20.20-23; Jn. 5.44).

In place of this prevailing world order Jesus announced the reign of God's Kingdom, a vision of the world in which relationships are rearranged and broadened: the addictive sentiments of familism, false patriotism, tribalism and nationalism were exposed and broken (Mk. 3.31-35; Lk. 11.27-28); the false promises of wealth, power, status and popularity were revealed for what they are (Mt. 19.23-26; I Jn. 2.16); a new center for human authenticity and social order was founded on the gift of self: it is in dying to the self that life is gained (Mt. 16.24-25). The death happens when we subject our egoistic tendencies (and that of the groups we belong to) to the judgment of God's unconditional love and the Christian values deriving from it. For instance, a priest who refuses to manipulate accounts (because he knows it is wrong) notwithstanding his own monetary needs and the encouragement of those who see nothing wrong with that, is attending to the Christian value of honesty and accountability. The life that is gained is not just the eternal life in heaven; it is also the experience of human authenticity and fulfilment and the progress of society because the common good is genuinely sought without jeopardy to the good of the individual. In this vision of life, we make choices and decisions based on what is good, what is true and worthwhile and not merely on what pleases us or the members of our family or ethnic group or nation. It is when many of us have learned to do this that "we can be principles of benevolence and beneficence, capable of genuine collaboration and of true love"[2].

As a member and an apostle of this new world order inaugurated by Jesus Christ, the priest embodies in himself and in what he does this new vision of life, its meaning and dynamics. Though it is the vision shared and lived by all Christians, we priests should live it out more intensely because of our leadership position in the Church. Inserted in this vision of life, we are in the forefront of a rescue operation which starts with ourselves: setting human beings free from the prison of their individual egoism and the oppressive structures erected by the accumulated history of egoism of groups, tribes, and nations. We must not merely know the nature of this new world order intellectually (which is what we study in theology); we should experience its liberating force in ourselves by consciously engaging ourselves with it. This demands a conscious decision to apply ourselves fully to our being as priests[3].

Now, if we priests, who are inserted in this new world order and are publicly known to be its champion and propagator, live according to the principles of the prevailing world order, we are headed for serious trouble with ourselves and with society. We live a theoretical contradiction that is reflected often in the inconsistencies in our attitudes and behaviour. In the contradictions of our life, we might fight consciously or unconsciously the vision of life that we both represent and embody.

It is in the context of this vision of life, this new world order, that the gospel counsels should be presented and understood. When seen in this perspective, they cease to be isolated disciplines to be taken but a manner of life embodied in this vision of life.

The Kingdom Incarnated: the Gospel Counsels

The counsels of the gospel make deeper sense, because they constitute the concrete manner in which the new world order inaugurated and embodied in Jesus Christ is expressed. Though the counsels express the radical commitment expected of every Christian without exception since all are called to holiness[4], it holds with a particular urgency for us priests. The basic reason is that our radical configuration to Christ places us in a special relationship to the Church, the Spouse of Christ[5]. This radical life of the gospel is expressed by the evangelical counsels of obedience, celibate chastity and poverty.

It is sometimes argued that these counsels are meant for the religious men and women and, in a lesser degree, for the diocesan priests. It is an impression created by the fact that religious life is traditionally associated with the evangelical counsels. But they are the counsels of the Christian faith. As Lane argues, "each of the evangelical counsels is undivided and it is inseparable from the other counsels". The counsels work together and their goal is to facilitate interior and exterior freedom in the Christian, without which it would be too difficult for the Christian to live a life of charity. A closer examination reveals that "this freeing, perfect charity and consecration which are normally associated with religious life, are, in fact, as much a programme for the lifestyle of the diocesan priest as they are for the religious. Common life, simple lifestyle, asceticism and austerity must keep finding their meaning in the working out of the programme of each"[6].

These counsels express how Jesus lived his life, his self-emptying in love of his Father and of us his brothers and sisters. Thus, they have their foundation in Jesus Christ and their manifestation in ministry, in pastoral activities[7]. Together, the gospel counsels express that fundamental obedience of faith in which "a man denies himself, renounces sin, selfishness, concupiscence, inordinate trust in his own strength, and yields himself to the merciful and loving God, confident in his forgiveness"[8]. I will now reflect on each of these three counsels and how they express the way we should live our lives to experience meaning or meaninglessness.

Willing Obedience

The use of the phrase "willing obedience" is important. Obedience is willing if it engages the freedom of the priest. It is indicated by the *conviction* with which the priest lives his obedience. If obedience becomes "unwilling", it can be lived as an imposition. In that sense, willing obedience is obedience that is responsible. When obedience is willing, it makes the persons who obey responsible for their lives. With human beings, any act of imposition, real or imagined, could be fought against actively or passively. I shall elaborate on this in the subsequent paragraphs. Let me first of all bring out what the Church teaches about this counsel.

It does not seem to be a mere coincidence that both the Second Vatican Council in its Decree on the Ministry and Life of Priests, *Presbyterorum Ordinis*, and John Paul II's post-synodal apostolic exhortation, *Pastores Dabo Vobis*, begin the treatment of the evangelical counsels with the counsel of obedience[9]. Obedience seems to occupy a central place because it expresses "that disposition of soul by which priests are always ready to seek not their own will, but the will of him who sent them"[10]. Theologically, obedience depicts the essence of ministry in the Church: the primacy of obedience to the God who calls and sends[11]. In that case, celibate chastity and poverty become further expressions of our radical disposition to seek and obey God's will in our lives.

The Decree on the Ministry and Life of Priests, *Presbyterorum Ordinis*, treats obedience together with humility. This linkage appears to be intentional. Obedience and humility bring out the need for us priests to acknowledge "the clay" that is our humanity through which the power of God manifests itself (II Cor. 4:7). In humility, we acknowledge the possibility of error in our own judgments and our need to be open for direction. As the Igbo proverb admonishes: *Agwo otu onye huru aghaghi igho eke* (A snake seen by one man might turn out to be a python). This proverb suggests the need for consultation and openness to other points of view.

This humble awareness of our humanity helps us to see the need to live the "willing obedience", which is that constant readiness to do the will of God as Christ did; the disposition "to find out what is well-pleasing to God"[12], and to see that our mission and projects express the mission of the Church. Concretely, the counsel of obedience is realized in two ways: first, when we accept in faith the assignments given to us by constituted authority in the Church, e.g., the Pope, the bishops or other superiors. Second, it also means that we should give ourselves totally and spend ourselves[13] in the assignments given to us. Wulf sees these two aspects of priestly obedience as summed up in "*sentire cum Ecclesia* and to hold oneself in ever greater readiness to work for the Church"[14]. These two aspects of obedience express our willingness as priests to submit our judgment to the appropriate authority for further discernment. This is also a concrete sign of communion with our superiors and with the members of the presbyterium, for "faithfulness to Christ cannot be separated from faithfulness to his Church"[15].

The Problematic in Obedience

Obedience is generally understood in terms of obeying the decisions of a bishop or the superior of a religious congregation as representing God's will for us. While it is true that the bishop or the superior listens to the intimations of the Holy Spirit in a particular decision process and makes decisions based on that, it is also true that some decisions are based on hunches, and sometimes on mere exercise of power. For this reason, some priests obey with ease and some others find it difficult to give their will either to God or to their superior, even though they are priests. For some others, they feel they owe obedience only to their own personal desires and interests and, so, make fun of gospel-obedience.

The evangelical counsel of obedience expresses that continuous readiness of both superiors and subordinates to seek and to carry out the will of God in their lives as Christ lived so that the reign of God is advanced in their own lives and among human beings. Experience shows that obedience can be abused by both superiors and subordinates. This happens whenever it is invoked by persons in positions of authority to dominate others and make them seem unthinking and worthless. Such interpretation and understanding of gospel-obedience gratifies hard-hearted superiors for whom power and control of others is more important than knowing Jesus Christ. It promotes unhealthy submissiveness in some persons, especially those with personality traits that incline them to want others to make decisions for them. It also increases the number of aggressive individuals who resist both imagined and real signs of command. Gospel-obedience is also abused when self-willed priests insist on having their way in everything and every time. Such priests suspect that any refusal to their self-willed projects and desires is a sign of oppression and should be fought with a stronger assertion of self-will. These priests usually find it difficult to deal with authority[16].

Gospel-obedience makes one responsible and not stupid or irresponsible. Responsible obedience to persons in authority should be able to engage the freedom of priests so that they (the priests) can offer their obedience willingly, because they are offering it to God in imitation of Jesus Christ. In the same way, priests should be able to respect those entrusted into their care, whether in the parish or in the school or in administration, as persons who think and reflect. Responsible obedience is able to confront the false assumption behind unruly self-will, which insists that the best way to live is to have what one desires, when and how one wants it, irrespective of standards of judgment and existential circumstances. This can be found in both superiors and subordinates, though its manifestation is different in each of them. This arrogant assertion of self-will is the greatest obstacle to living out the counsel of obedience. In fact, it is the greatest obstacle to any serious following of Jesus Christ, our Lord and Master. The reason is because such an attitude tends to neglect the impact of the life and values of Jesus Christ in the transformation of our desires and choices.

That gospel-obedience should be responsible or willing is founded on the fact that human beings are endowed with the capacity to make decisions and choices and to follow a reasonable project of life. This ability to decide freely is a primary act of being human. It explains why there is always an almost instinctive rebelliousness in human beings toward any kind of real or imagined imposition, be it from a fellow man or even from God. It is as if the sound of a command triggers off a corresponding reaction to it. All totalitarian governments where people are forced to accept certain beliefs and way of life to which they do not consent; all situations of domination and subjugation, whether overt or covert; all relationships that tend to engulf persons or that are structured in master-slave form, are bound to hatch overt and covert rebels, passive aggressive attitudes and/or pathologically dependent persons or groups. These are instances of irresponsible compulsion in the name of obedience. Because they are sometimes present in the priesthood and the religious life, individuals with passive aggressive attitudes have been found to be in great number[17].

By their nature, human beings resent being commanded unnecessarily without understanding. They want to understand because they possess intelligence; they want to be understood because they should be respected for whom they are as persons. When they understand and are understood, they can give their consent fully and are motivated to carry out what is asked of them to the best of their capacity. This understanding is respect; it is love, and whenever it is present, even if the situation is not understood clearly, the individual can still offer his consent. This is evident in the way God deals with us.

Jesus woos men and women to life; he persuades them to see with him; he tries to understand each person in his or her situation; he lets each person experience his love. In doing that, he attracts them to himself, and, in attracting them, he energizes them to follow him. Thus, when a man is secure in the love of God manifest in Jesus Christ, he is ready to go miles with him even under the burden of all the interior resistances.

The *Spiritual Exercises* of St. Ignatius of Loyola is structured in this manner. The retreatant is first introduced to the love of God that reaches its definitive form in the person of Jesus Christ. Realizing how God loves him, the retreatant looks back to see how badly he has been living; how he has been hurting love and hurting himself. This usually leads the person to a confession of sins and a decision to live a better life of obedience to God. It is then that the person hands his or her life over to Jesus to direct, and this consists in listening and obeying his inspirations in order to deepen the relationship between them. Obedience to God in Jesus Christ has become the foundation of the person's life in all circumstances. In those dark moments of faith when life is tough and circumstances refuse to make sense, it is this love, this faith in the compassion and understanding of Jesus, which sees the person through. The Ignatian insight which is structured in the *Spiritual Exercises* remains valid through the centuries because it expresses the dynamics of the relationship of love between us and God, and how, through this love, God transforms us.

Obedience is responsible when it forms the orientation of our whole life in imitation of the obedience of Christ, in total self-giving that is not resentful. Single acts of obedience coming from this basic disposition always lead us closer to the heart of Jesus and to our own fulfilment as human beings and as priests. Hence, every genuine act of gospel-obedience brings greater interior freedom that we all need to give ourselves to God and to the service of His people. If our acts of gospel-obedience do not do that, they may be serving some other purpose other than this. They could be expressions of the immature areas of personality rather than of the gospel value of obedience. For such persons, obedience is attractive as a value because it gratifies their need for either domination as an authority or submissiveness and rebelliousness as a subordinate. Superiors and subordinates with disorders of personality can so easily manifest these attitudes.

Celibate Chastity

The Church makes effort to help us understand priestly celibacy as rooted in our relationship with Christ. It symbolizes that pastoral charity by which we priests totally and with undivided heart, give ourselves to God in the service of the people of God[18]; it is the gift of ourselves "*in* and *with* Christ *to* his Church and expresses the priest's service to the Church in and with the Lord"[19]. At the heart of priestly celibacy is Jesus Christ, the High Priest of the New Testament, whom we represent sacramentally. Just as Christ wholly dedicated his life to God and to his mission and chose to remain celibate throughout his life, so the priest, called by Christ to continue His mission, is also invited to dedicate his whole life to Him and to His mission. This is the ultimate reason why the Church links celibacy to the priesthood[20]. Viewed this way, priestly celibacy becomes a sign of our total disposition to love Christ and his Church without reservation[21].

We live out our celibate chastity in our relationship with ourselves, with God, and with others. It does not mean remaining unmarried or single for pastoral efficiency. Some priests tend to see priestly celibacy simply as remaining unmarried, a bachelor. The reason for this is probably because priestly celibacy is often taken to be a matter of Church discipline enacted for pragmatic purposes, that is, for pastoral efficiency[22]. Though this reasoning goes back to the origin of priestly celibacy in the Latin Church, experience has taught everyone that such discipline could be inhuman. I personally feel repulsed by that idea. Gallagher and Vandenberg are correct when they observe that "if all that can be said in favour of celibacy is that it frees the priest to work more for the institutional Church, that in fact is an admission that celibacy is exploitative and cruel"[23]. It is cruel and exploitative precisely because "neither marriage nor celibacy is livable without a commitment of love so deep as to cause one to want to give up all else"[24]. Such an undertaking without a "love so deep" can crush the person himself and those around him because it is psychologically destructive. Therefore, celibacy is not meant to be perpetual bachelorhood for pastoral efficiency but a relationship with, and love for Christ and for the Church. It is chosen "in order that we may live more a life totally dependent on faith in love so that we may be a concentrated and visible sign of faith, of adhesion to the Lord"[25]. Celibate chastity of the priest is "an affirmation that God's reign is a higher value than any other value, even the most marvellous human love between a man and a woman"[26]; therefore, it is a sign that "a man has staked his whole life on God"[27].

The motivation for priestly celibacy is fundamentally religious: united with Christ in this love, this manner of life enables us to give ourselves continuously to God and to humanity. Thus, the emphasis is not on remaining single or unmarried and has nothing to do with rigid attitudes of Manichaeism or Stoicism[28].

The Danger of Living Celibacy as a Law

The Church acknowledges that celibacy for us priests of the Latin Church is a law that was made sometime in history. From that time till today, the teaching authority of the Church has consistently confirmed this decision and expressed no wish for it to be removed[29]. At the same time, the Church realizes that celibacy itself is not essentially connected to the ordained ministry[30]. In the theology of the priesthood from Vatican II till date, efforts have been made to reconcile these two issues, the ordained ministry *and* the gift of celibacy. The link is found in Jesus Christ, who is the high priest of the new dispensation, who gave himself totally to God for the salvation of humanity. Thus, the celibacy of the ordained priesthood is founded on the love of Jesus Christ for which the priest could give up everything to be internally and externally free to serve God's people as Jesus Christ did.

This placement of priestly celibacy in the context of love of Jesus makes sense psychologically. It is this psychological implication that I wish to pursue in this section since celibacy is still required for all those who feel called to the ordained ministry in the Latin Church.

It is my opinion, backed by personal experience and the experiences gained in clinical practice and spiritual direction, that as long as the tendency to emphasise the celibacy of the ordained priesthood in legal terms prevails either in theology or in personal convictions of individual priests, there will be serious problems both for the Church and for the priests themselves. This emphasis on celibacy as law could make some priests see their lives as an unbearable sacrifice, so that some are angry that their life is a burden. Some put on long faces and furrowed brows, unconsciously though, for people to have pity on them. For some others, celibacy means to remain single, and this may or may not include chastity. This usually implies that if they live unchaste lives, it is their entitlement and not a sin of which to be repented. These two positions are equally dangerous: the one could lead to an unhappy and meaningless life in which one feels cheated and always angry; the other could lead to a careless and irresponsible lifestyle that may include various forms of sexual exploitation and abuse. The accumulated result of such a manner of living could be experience of confusion and meaninglessness.

When celibacy is largely understood in terms of denial of sex, formation could mean giving the candidates the techniques and methods of keeping themselves 'neat' from being soiled sexually. Priests so trained could spend more time preoccupied with being 'neat' and unsoiled than they devote to deepening their knowledge of Jesus Christ and their relationship with him.

Other problems arise from taking priestly celibacy as merely legal. First, it can make the priest tend to see himself as a functionary, one who merely discharges the duties assigned to him; this may not necessarily affect the way he lives his life as long as he remains celibate, unmarried. This internal division between his pastoral activities and his private life could give him the room to engage in sexual exploits with or without remorse, depending on his personality. In this regard, Osborn observes that "an emphasis on the legal connection of celibacy to the ordained ministry has very serious ethical implications, implications which revolve around the distinction of what is merely legal and what is both illegal and immoral"[31]. This problem would not exist whenever a priest lived his celibacy as a relationship of love with Jesus Christ and the Church.

Secondly, priestly vocation could be easily transformed into a project of achievement so that one substitutes intimacy with God and persons with the desire for power and control. Such priests may not be worried about their sexual life and may not be interested in intimate relationships because all energy is invested in the search for positions of power and visible signs of achievement. Lacking real intimacy either with persons or with God, priestly authority could be turned into a ruthless exercise of power that hurts people as much as it abuses them.

Even if the celibacy of the ordained ministry has a legal aspect, it need not be emphasised, for the wellbeing of the priest and of the Church. If one merely enters into marriage only on the requirements of marital validity provided by the Canon Law, the marriage may be valid, but it may not be fulfilling. The couple should be able to develop and nurture sincere love for one another and for their children. This is what guides them through the ups and downs of their life-long commitment.

The same applies to us celibate priests. We are persons who have encountered the love of God in fact and not in theory. It is this love that enables us to go through the joyful and sorrowful moments of our life without resentment or grudges. It is this love which gives meaning and direction to our sexual energies. In nurturing this selfless love between us and Jesus Christ and the Church, we grow in our humanity and in our vocation.

Maloney argues this point on a different plane. The starting point of his argument is the rejection, on the basis of biblical scholarship, of the traditional foundation of celibate chastity on Jesus statement in Mt. 19.12: "Some are incapable of marriage because they were born so; some, because they were made so by others; some, because they have renounced marriage for the sake of the Kingdom of God". According to him, this passage of the scripture occurred in the context of the abuses which Jesus' enemies were heaping on him. Just like the African cultures, Jewish culture could not understand a man who chose not to marry and have his own children. In fact, to call someone eunuch was a caricature. It was actually used for people who were physically incapable of marrying and having children. And there are just two categories of such people: those who are eunuch by nature *and* those made so by men. Thus, according to Maloney, "it seems that another term used to attack Jesus was 'Eunuch!'"[32]. He further explains that "Matt. 19.12 on the lips of Jesus was his calm reply to the attacks from his enemies who sought any excuse to hurl abuse at this troublesome character. Jesus was a celibate, and was thus immediately open to such abuse, particularly as he was a public figure who troubled the establishment by the quality and authority of his life and preaching. I would suggest that one of the reasons why this particular 'word of Jesus' remained alive in the tradition, despite the harshness of the word, 'eunuch', was because it was Jesus' regular answer to a regular form of abuse which was aimed at him"[33].

Maloney insists that Jesus accepted he was a celibate *because of* the kingdom of heaven. "He was not a celibate 'so that' he might construct the Kingdom, but 'because of' the overwhelming presence of the Kingdom"[34]. This means that the principal motive of Jesus' celibacy, against the caricature of his enemies, was not simply physical like the condition of eunuchs by nature or those made so by men. The main point is that Jesus "was taken over by the urgent presence of the Kingdom that he could do no other than give himself entirely to it. The celibacy of Jesus was not something which he made happen to himself by first deliberating whether or not it should happen, and then deciding in favour of it so that he would be free to dedicate himself entirely to the construction of the Kingdom. The causality ran in the opposite direction. In Jesus of Nazareth the guiding principle and the overwhelming experience of his life was the presence of the lordship of God whom he called 'Father'. It was this 'lordship' which led him to his state of celibacy, to his being a eunuch *because of* the overwhelming presence of the Kingdom in his life ..."[35].

Maloney therefore gives a solid conclusion that agrees with the psychospiritual intuition which I emphasise here, that only on the basis of a love so deep could the commitment of marriage and celibacy be lived without complexes. In his own words: "Like Jesus, we are chaste because of the overwhelming presence of God's Kingdom which keeps crowding in on us. In other words, our ongoing decision for chastity is intelligible as a decision which comes about within the context of a major religious experience, just as the decision for marriage comes about within the context of a major religious experience. A life of chastity is nothing else but the existential consequence which flows out of the prior experience of the urgent presence of the Kingdom of God. This is what it means to be 'a eunuch for the sake of the Kingdom of heaven'"[36].

In psychological language, this breaking in of the kingdom of heaven on the individual is an experience of love, and the response of vocation is the journey to deeper intimacy between the person and God. Celibacy in this context cannot be reduced to mere sexual continence or efforts to avoid sexual temptation. The fundamental temptation would be the betrayal of this unique relationship between the individual and God.

This has profound implication for the formation of celibate priests or religious men and women. Since celibacy was traditionally understood in terms of "freedom for the work of the kingdom", it usually happens that formation for celibacy turns out to be a conditioning process in which persons are drilled on how to acquire certain attitudes and mannerisms to keep them away from falling into sexual temptation. Experience shows that such efforts could be counterproductive and in many cases lead to certain forms of pathologies such as rigidity in relationship and obsession with sexual matters. In situations of serious stress, these pathological conditions could lead to violent sexual acting out. Living celibacy in this framework can be terribly frustrating and somehow meaningless. Formation for celibate life should focus more on the importance of intimacy, self-knowledge, and openness to genuine friendship. These constitute necessary aspects of our human maturity.

Voluntary Poverty

The third Gospel counsel is voluntary poverty by which priests "become more clearly conformed to Christ and more ready to devote themselves to their sacred ministry"[37]. Evangelical poverty helps to free the priest from unnecessary encumbrances that might suffocate the Spirit of God in him and enables him to cultivate that inner readiness to be sent on a mission anytime, anywhere. The interior freedom acquired from the practice of evangelical poverty makes the priest a trustworthy ally of the poor, the underprivileged, the oppressed, and all those who live on the margins of society.

The value of evangelical poverty has two dimensions: the pastoral and the prophetic[38]. In the pastoral dimension, the priest identifies with and cares for the poor and the weak. He does so by assuming a simple lifestyle, generously renouncing superfluous things, and by avoiding any kind of arrogant display of wealth or vanity that may antagonize or scandalize the poor[39]. It also entails that the priest should be honest in administering the temporal goods of the Church. A priest can be dishonest in two ways: first, when he takes the priestly office as an avenue to make profit and thus engages himself in different types of opportunistic self-aggrandisement; secondly, when he consciously and irresponsibly spends the money accruing from the office sometimes without proper accountability. In either case, it is avarice that is at work and it contradicts the value of priestly poverty.

The poverty of the priest is also prophetic: it is a witness to the contemporary world where money and affluence have become the yardsticks for measuring personal worth and relevance[40]. In living a simple lifestyle, the priest points to God and His Kingdom as the more genuine and authentic security[41]. It does not mean that the priest will have to live in substandard conditions; he should live in conditions worthy of human beings. The guiding principle remains that he should be able to make the *right use of things* in the *light of the Gospel*. Using this principle of the Christian faith, priests will be ready "to reject anything that is prejudicial to their mission"[42].

Assured Security and the Problem of Insensitivity

The Gospel counsel of poverty expresses three ideas: first, it is a training in a simple lifestyle which is dependent on God's providential care. Secondly, it points to our responsibility towards each other in sharing what we have – material and immaterial. Finally, this counsel also expresses our existential poverty, the poverty of our being, the realization of which should humble us.

First and foremost, Gospel poverty implies a lifestyle that exposes and expresses our relationship with God as both the core and the direction of our life as priests. It is largely based on an acute awareness of what is necessary for a decent life and service of God and what is superfluous. The Church wants a decent life for her priests, and the lay faithful do everything possible to make their priests comfortable. In most places of the Catholic world, priests, religious and diocesan, belong to that class of people with a relatively good socio-economic security. This kind of assured security should be an avenue for us priests *to choose* to live a simple lifestyle that expresses our singular love for God and readiness to share with the people we serve. On the basis of that kind of life, we can ally with the weak and the poor in working for a better society with greater opportunity for everyone; we can also direct people to the experience of freedom from unnecessary superfluities in their lives, so as to learn to share with others; and, we can be sensitive to the poor conditions of some of the people we serve.

Simplicity of life goes hand in hand with inner readiness to share ourselves, what we have and are, with others. What we have does not have to be material; our gifts and talents should be shared. The disposition to share everything we have derives from our keen awareness that all life is a gift to be shared and not to be possessed just for one's personal satisfaction. In sharing our gifts, we are enriched, and we enrich others. This idea of poverty captures the scriptural understanding of mutual responsibility towards each other and towards the world, because we are all children of God and co-creators with God in renewing the world and making it a better place.

It is sometimes the case that some of us priests, breathing the air of assured security, let themselves indulge their desires and cravings with a kind of stoic insensitivity to the condition of people who support them. We grow to be very selfish and unfeeling about the situation around us. In our comfort, we are desensitized from the deplorable situation of the world. In many countries where the majority of the population is poor, it is not unusual to see, for instance, priests who have two or three personal cars, in addition to the parish car. It is not that they *need* these cars in many of the instances; it is often a gratification of a desire to belong to a class. These three cars are maintained from the parish fund. There are also those who throw parties in the rectory always, again, from the parish fund. But there are children in those parishes who cannot go to school for lack of money; there are persons who cannot afford to pay their hospital bills!

Assured security can harden hearts so that such persons are unable to feel the painful condition of others, lest, perhaps, they be disturbed in their comfort. It is not unusual to find priests with hard hearts in both rich and poor countries. In the rich countries of Europe and North America, the security of the rectory could make priests insensitive to the people's struggle with job insecurities and the payment for utilities. In poor countries, assured security tends to create a bourgeois class that inoculates itself against the suffering faces and surroundings.

This insensitivity reaches its high point in those smug attitudes of entitlement. An example: a story was told of a priest in Nigeria who refused to celebrate mass for the parishioners during the time of fuel scarcity. What was his reason? The parishioners could not buy him the fuel he needed to operate the generator in the rectory, which he needed to watch his cable television and play his brass music. This was the time when the scarcity of fuel was an additional pain and suffering to the people. But the priest was insensitive to it – for the sake of indulging his cravings and desires. Insensitive attitude is the easiest way we priests can work against the very gospel we preach; the gospel that presents God as our true security. The scandalous affluence of some of us priests and our insensitivity to the plight of the people is one of the greatest insinuators of people's anger toward us today. But it all starts from the assured security of the priestly "poverty".

To live meaningfully, each of us has got to negotiate personally with the assured security that seems to be part of the priestly life. Each person must make a conscious decision to live a simple lifestyle that flows from his deep relationship with our Lord and the Church, or a life of self-indulgence.

The final aspect of the gospel poverty is the existential one. This aspect is hardly mentioned in this counsel. The reason is because poverty evokes material indigence, and our attention easily goes to the people at the margins of society. This tends to distract us from having to face the poverty of human condition, which is expressed in our own lives and personalities: the disorders we encounter in ourselves, different degrees of powerlessness, the sins and habits we struggle with everyday, our various obsessions. These experienced incapacities and vulnerabilities become occasions of genuine humility and candid admission of the need for grace in one's life. Our priesthood therefore does not set us apart as if we are out of touch with the struggles of human beings; it rather brings us face to face with it. From the experience of our poor humanities and of the power of God's redemptive love, we can become better witnesses of the Living God. This aspect of Gospel poverty indeed rescues us from the tendency to feel superior over others simply because we minister to them. It humbles us and gives us the concrete chance to take on the mind of Christ who, though he was divine, humbled himself and became one like us.

Priestly Life is a System of Meaning

The Christian vision of life, which is clearly expressed in the dynamic counsels of the Gospel, makes priestly life a system of meaning for the priest. Like all human beings, we seek for the meaning of our lives. The desire for the meaning of our lives covers all that we are and do. When we feel that our lives make sense, we are motivated to live, to act, to work, to decide, to relate, to worship, to suffer, to bear with others, and to engage in any other experience of the human being. The yearning for this purposeful living may not be completely articulated by many persons, but it remains the basis of all human struggles and activities such that the concrete experiences of human doubts, worries, preoccupations, skepticisms, nausea, are necessary means that induce each person to seek the experience of his or her deepest self in its ultimate destiny.

Christian life is a system of meaning that offers Christians a veritable framework for understanding and interpreting life as a whole, and their own lives in particular. From this framework, they derive the norms of their moral and social lives, and give their concrete choices and decisions some coherence around Christian ideals.

By virtue of our vocation as priests, we embody this Christian worldview in our persons. We are persons who *know* the structure of human existence as needing and searching for meaning; and have *experienced* in our own persons the disquiet of the human spirit in its search for meaning and purpose; and have *found the answer* in the religious domain, incarnated in the life of Jesus Christ and of the Church. From this domain we seek to understand the destiny of human life and all human struggles and efforts. We are in touch with the agitations of the human heart, which is reflected in the disorder and agitations of human societies and relationships, and we have veritable response in the life and ministry of Jesus Christ and the Church. Without such knowledge of our own self, of our inner desires, search and disquiet, and of the meaning that the personal experience of God in Jesus Christ brings, we could be mere mercenaries and the priesthood a mere career. This attitude is dangerous to our existence as priests, and has serious negative effects in the pastoral ministry. I shall elaborate on this fully in the last chapter.

Synthesis

In the concrete life of priests, intellectual knowledge of the elements of priestly identity would not be complete unless each priest recognises and engages himself with the dialectic inherent in priestly vocation. That dialectic is already present in the Christian vision of life, but is expressed concretely in the life of the priest in this manner: our ministry as priests makes a special claim on us not to conform to the world; yet, it requires at the same time that we should live among people in this world and, as good shepherds, we should know the flock entrusted into our care[43]. Expressed differently, we priests are servants of Christ, and witnesses and dispensers of a life beyond this earth, the vision of life that is Christian. At the same time, we would be powerless to serve people if we "remained aloof from their life and circumstances"[44]. As priests, therefore, we move between heaven and earth, between what is not seen and what is seen. We give witness to the heavenly reality, but are rooted on earth. In order to manage this dialectic well, it is important that we grow and mature in our vocation. That is to say, the fact of being a priest should occupy the center of our motivational system and become the origin and end of our decisions and choices. This is the foundation of our fulfilment as priests. Otherwise, we would be chasing shadows and experiencing emptiness and meaninglessness. In the chapter that follows, I shall explore how this dialectic expresses itself in our lives and how it is related to our experience of fulfilment and non-fulfilment.

Chapter Three

Searching for Fulfilment: Satisfied and Dissatisfied Priests

If one is a Catholic priest but does not honestly desire and sincerely make effort to live as one, he may become sad and unhappy irrespective of his position in the Church and his possessions. What has been said in the last two chapters is the foundation of the priests' experience of satisfaction or dissatisfaction, that is, meaning or meaninglessness, in their lives. In chapter one, I explored the theological and psychological foundations on which authentic priestly life depends. In chapter two, I examined the vision of life underlying the priestly vocation, which is expressed in the Gospel counsels.

Priesthood can be a joyful and meaningful life for some priests as well as a burden and misery for others. A priest for whom the priesthood is satisfying and fulfilling comes across as one whose presence brings peace, encouragement, and motivation for living. When a priest is unfulfilled or dissatisfied with his life, his presence can be irritating; he is unsettled and in constant search for fulfilment such that he may keep looking for satisfaction in wrong places and in things that may not be helpful. An unfulfilled person is hardly consoled by life, and may be erratic in pursuit of what may be felt to be too far from the horizon. In the frantic search for happiness and fulfilment, the status of the priesthood could be used to cause harm to himself and to others.

It is the search for satisfaction in life that leads some priests to adopt a style of life that appears anything but simple, unassuming, and interiorly secured. For the same reason, some seem to be too ready to indulge themselves in many forms that put to question the authenticity of their priestly status in society. Others live in constant anticipation that life is more fulfilling on the other side of the fence. The source of such anticipation is often the experience of dissatisfaction or meaninglessness in life.

Human experience shows that some people are satisfied and others are dissatisfied in their lives. For instance, one may be married but remains unfulfilled as a married person. Such a person may find his or her fulfilment more in work than in the marital life[1]. A practical consequence of this psychological condition is that one may tend to pay greater attention to work than to family life, such that both spousal and parental relationships are endangered. Secondly, it is possible that the individual experiences serious conflicts within, which may lead eventually to divorce, having an affair, or neglect of the family. Among priests, such experience of serious internal conflicts could lead to acting out that could be criminal or to aberrant behaviours that, though not obviously criminal, may be morally distasteful and existentially self-defeating. It is then that the roles and the status of the priesthood could be employed by the priest in service of his personal satisfaction, and he may cause harm to people and himself in this process.

So, why are some priests satisfied or fulfilled and others dissatisfied or unfulfilled in their lives? What could be the source of satisfaction and dissatisfaction in the priesthood? Before we can address this question, we need to examine what life-satisfaction or self-fulfilment means, and how it relates to priestly existence.

Being Satisfied/Fulfilled as a Priest

Levels of Satisfaction in Life

The word "satisfaction" may be understood at three levels at which human beings generally live, namely, the psychobiological, the psychosocial, and the psychospiritual. First, the word is used to refer to that experience in which a particular biological need is gratified, as when one satisfies the need of thirst with a cold bottle of soft drink and expresses his satisfaction with an 'aha'! At this first level, satisfaction largely applies to the biological equilibrium that is reestablished when the tension created by a need is removed.

At the psychosocial level, satisfaction depicts "an emotional state produced by achieving some goal"[2], as when one passes an exam or successfully organizes a conference or a bazaar. At this level also we can speak of the satisfaction that comes from doing something well so that people are appreciative of it. For instance, one is satisfied when one is a well-known fundraiser, a good organizer, a good teacher, a good preacher, a good counselor, a good administrator. But one may have received praises for being a good teacher, a well-spoken professor, a wonderful preacher, an important scholar, but still feels empty and restless as a person, which could drive him to seek for more of such praises.

Hence there is a third and deeper level at which human beings experience satisfaction: it is the psychospiritual level, that symbolic universe of human beings[3], where we raise the central question of the meaning of our lives. Satisfaction here expresses one's affective stance before life as a whole; it is that state of contentment and well-being, an affective state in which one feels that one's life makes sense, that all one does and is fall in place within a project of life. This fundamental satisfaction is what is generally referred to as fulfillment or meaning in life. This last sense of satisfaction relates to the being of the person, to what the person is, essentially, a person's identity:

a married person, a priest, a religious, or a single person. And here, we can begin to see how one's experience of being a priest is related to one's experience of satisfaction or dissatisfaction.

Temporary and Life-Satisfaction

Temporary satisfaction or sporadic excitement expresses the satisfaction we experience at the psychobiological and psychosocial levels such as when we fill our stomachs with food or when we bask in the admiration of people. But the satisfaction at these two levels does not address the deeper yearning for fulfilment, for a life that makes sense. The reason is because the human being is not merely material and social; he is also spiritual. He will remain restless until he situates his specific strivings within this one fundamental striving for meaning or fulfilment. No matter how we satisfy our physical and social needs, we still thirst and ache for meaning or fulfilment. This is the deepest aspiration of being human. This meaning, this spiritual aspiration in our hearts, is what the values of Jesus Christ, the values of the Christian vocation, of priestly vocation, seek to respond to. As priests, we begin to experience this deep fulfilment, of the meaning of our life, when we strive to appropriate the total meaning of priestly identity. The priest who takes good doses of temporary satisfaction – at the first and second levels of satisfaction – remains dissatisfied; he will still yearn for the deeper satisfaction that subsumes these other ones. The desire for this deeper satisfaction often comes strongly to the consciousness at one time or another in our life's journey. In some people it begins early, while in others it comes later. Such is the moment in our life when we can no longer escape the basic question: where is my life heading to? Where has all this led me? What meaning has my life?

These questions do not mean that our contributions to the Church and society are meaningless. They rather suggest that the contributions have served the world but may not have helped us experience the depth of life, because they may have been means of escape from the true self. Thus a priest may be an acclaimed professor, scholar, writer, fundraiser, builder, preacher, healer, a seasoned parish priest, but may wind up in depression, hopelessness, regrets, agitation, frustration, and emptiness. Some try to avoid the questions through drinking, sexual promiscuity, compulsive acquisition of money and material things, and even through living a noisy social life. Others make it a point of duty never to sit still in a place for a long time unless they are busy. Such are always on the road or in the midst of likeminded priests talking and drinking. There are also others who have withdrawn from active pursuit of these things, and have gone to sleep. All they do is seek maximum comfort: they sleep, drink, feed themselves and avoid the least inconveniences in their lives. But there comes a time in life when these persons will not be able again to escape through sleeping and drinking. In this group we find those priests who have lost the taste and drive for the priestly life and ministry and have learned to protect themselves from the demands of meaning through an attitude of indifference. Nothing seems to move or bother them; they pretend to float with life and do not want to be disturbed. But life also has a way of surprising such people and jerking them up from their protective apathy. And when this happens, their deep-seated dissatisfaction with life could be released with force that the person may be overwhelmed to the point of emotional breakdown.

These experiences and the frustrations they bring could be the occasion for the experience of grace, the realization that these petty satisfactions are no longer satisfying. If the message of the frustrations is not understood, they can become destructive to the person and even to the church and society[4].

All this is meant to demonstrate that our authentic satisfaction, our true self-fulfilment as priests, lies in living an intimacy with Jesus that finds expression outside in the apostolate. It is an ongoing process, which is verified in the increasing acquisition of the willingness to make a gift of ourselves in each circumstance of our lives in response to the love of Jesus and for humanity. This willingness is that inner disposition we develop by which we no longer need to be persuaded to know or believe that in the selfless path traced by Jesus and the values he taught and lived lie the transformation of our person, the meaning of our lives, and the true foundation of authentic social order.

The implication of what has been said so far is that the true and lasting satisfaction that we seek as priests is dependent on two factors: first, on the awareness that our existence as priests makes sense within the vision inaugurated by Jesus Christ, which is the heart of the Christian mission. If we fundamentally live outside this vision, we are likely to suffer alienation both from our "self" and from society. If we realize where we belong and the vision of life that defines our existence, then the second factor is easy to understand, namely, the healthy management of discipleship and apostolate. Our life is a shuttle between heaven and earth; between intimacy with Jesus and service to the world; between our interior life and our involvement in society. We need to assume our proper place in this vision of life (discipleship, intimacy with Jesus) *in order* to be able to understand and address the alienating and oppressive structures that imprison individuals and groups (apostolate) with the message of the Gospel.

Fulfilment and the Integration of Discipleship and Apostolate

We noted earlier in chapter one that Catholic priesthood is not a profession or a career that one enters in order to realize his potentialities or live a life of comfort. The new world order, the vision of life of the Gospel, which is the Christian life in general and in which the priesthood is inserted, indicates that the priesthood is of a different order, the order of the spiritual, of discipleship, of self-gift, of an intense life of relationship of love with God in His Christ for the sake of the mission.

The identity of the priest is structured around two pillars, namely identification with Christ *and* mission. Concretely the one expresses a priest's closeness to and intimacy with Jesus Christ through the radical life of the gospel, and the other his apostolate. The priest lives "always between the mission of his office and the intimacy and demand of personal discipleship"[5]. He cultivates his relationship with Christ, and from the depth of his interiority, his intimacy with Jesus, he carries out his apostolate. The journey to the fullness of life in Jesus Christ as a priest takes place through an interior life and apostolate. But, between this interiority (discipleship) and the demands of apostolate, priests experience tension deriving mostly from their psychological dispositions. The personal relationship with Jesus Christ provides the background against which the priest assesses his own life and the motives behind the projects he carries out in his apostolate. Most of us priests will testify that whenever we pay casual attention to our relationship with Jesus, our effectiveness as priests is always affected. It is impossible to take one's discipleship seriously without effective apostolate. That is why all appearances of being prayerful without a corresponding expression of this prayerfulness through the apostolate are deceptive.

Some priests think themselves to be dutifully prayerful, but they are so overly concerned with their prayer that their apostolate is neglected. This kind of disposition leads to a kind of spiritualism or flight from the world. But it does not necessarily lead to closeness with Jesus Christ, which should be evident in lifestyle, relationship with people, and in the apostolate. Most of these priests often feel useless and interiorly angry because of a kind of ineptitude they exhibit towards their personal lives and the demands of the ministry. Somehow it would appear that their apparent prayerfulness is a kind of escape from the challenges of living. They could be lazy but may feel satisfied that people know them to be prayerful, that they do not mess up with 'the things of the world'. This feeling of satisfaction is temporary because it is associated mostly with the passing compliments of persons. Prayerful attitude, in this sense, is being *used* to serve or cover up a feeling of insecurity. Priests in this group may be few.

A good number of us priests fall within the group of those who tend to emphasise their apostolate. This is the avenue that can so easily gratify our need for achievement and social recognition. In this way we easily make exhibition of our competence (efficiency). Such priests are inclined to identify the priesthood with the 'role' of the priest and neglect the interior dimension. In this group are those who tend *to use* the priesthood to promote their image and social status. They may vie for their 'favourite' apostolate for the honour and/or money that it promises. For instance, one may prefer to work in the university than in the seminary for the social status attached to it. Some want to work with and around the bishop, to be closer to power, in order to push forward their desires and ambitions and not necessarily to serve the Church. If they are in the parish, their reference point is always the number of buildings they erect and the amount of money they make for the parish and the diocese for which they should be recognised, and possibly be promoted. If these are not possible, they can become sad or disgruntled or feel worthless. There are those in this group for whom the means of achieving popularity and relevance is fighting with the real and imagined demons and unseen forces especially in our African milieu. Priestly apostolate is then narrowed to healing and deliverance sessions, and in putting up mystifying attitudes and behaviours. Exploiting the religious sensitivity of the people, these priests become the parameters of what it means to be the priest. In all this, the apostolate appears to be the driving force but it is covertly used to advance one's name, image, popularity, status, extraordinariness and spiritual powers.

How are these efforts related to the experience of fulfilment or life-satisfaction? We need not argue about or question the validity of different apostolates and how they are related to the priestly discipleship. But we can ask ourselves personal questions such as these: does my assignment increase my love for Jesus and the people entrusted to me? Does my assignment bring me deep peace and joy? Am I really satisfied or fulfilled in my life as a priest or am I simply going through sporadic moments of excitement? These questions express a fundamental question in the life of every priest: is my satisfaction in life temporary or enduring?

Identity Confusion and the Uncertainty of Fulfilment

A primary source of non-satisfaction or dissatisfaction in the priestly life is vocational immaturity in its various aspects. Vocational immaturity has to do with a deep-seated difficulty in properly identifying the core of oneself as a priest. It expresses itself in many forms but especially in desire for something else other than *being* priest. This is the heart of priestly-identity crisis. The desire could be conscious or unconscious. Whether it is conscious or unconscious, the manifestation seems to take some patterns: excessive pursuit of power and control, undue attachment to the status and role of priests in society, strong desire for popularity that often leads some priests to manipulative activities that could be theologically questionable especially in our African Church. And so on. While these desires are present in each of us, they do not have to constitute the central driving force in our lives. When any of these desires becomes invested with intense motivational energy, they express a deep sense of lack in the priest's experience of himself as a priest, which is identity crisis or confusion. Such a person tends to be unsure or uncertain about his fulfilment as a priest. In the light of this, it is not difficult to see that maturity in one's vocation, that is, proper self-definition as a priest, brings satisfaction or life fulfilment to the person, and immaturity expresses itself as some lack in one's life that seeks to be fulfilled. The concepts of maturity and immaturity should not be conceived as static points of arrival in the human and vocational journey. They rather express our greater or lesser acquisition of our vocational identity as priests. The process of acquiring our vocational identity is a continuous one.

A priest who is reasonably mature in his vocation is happy generally and can handle most of the problems that he encounters; he does not feel that he will be happier or more satisfied if something is added to his being a priest. An illustration: a man who is mature in his gender identity is at home with himself, satisfied with his masculinity. The man who is not mature in his gender identity may tend to exaggerate his masculinity in order to impress or convince himself, perhaps subconsciously, that he is a complete man. This is a persistent source of anxiety and dissatisfaction in some men which, in extreme situations, could lead to cross-gender behaviours. What is being stated here is that immaturity in any area of a person's life could generate significant difficulties and dissatisfactions in that aspect of life. When one is immature in the central organising identity of one's life, then most of the person's life is affected: it is the deepest source of dissatisfaction and meaninglessness in life.

This implies that the degree of our vocational maturity could reflect the degree we experience fulfilment or non-fulfilment in our lives as priests, because vocational maturity entails a greater congruence between different aspects of the self. Immaturity, on the other hand, expresses some discrepancy in the self, and it is reflected in lack of inner security in the person's experience of life.

We grow in maturity the more we bring our thoughts, desires, needs and attitudes to reflect and express the values of our persons as priests. This means that we do our best to focus our desires and energies on our personal relationship with God and the service of the mission. The sincere effort and the perseverance to remain faithful to God and to the mission, despite failures, are our sources of deep joy and peace.

Immaturity dominates our lives as priests when most of what we do is serving our personal needs and interests, and worse, when they do not agree with the values of the priesthood. Here, we reinterpret the values of priestly vocation in such a way that we literally *use* the priesthood for *ourselves*, living it the way we feel and not the way we should. Our attitudes are then ambivalent, appearing to express the values of Jesus Christ but, in a real sense, we are serving our personal interests.

Now, all forms of conscious dishonesty toward one's vocation as a priest is not only a moral issue for the individual concerned, the church and the world, but existentially, it is a form of self-deception. When one, for instance, enters into the priesthood with the conscious motive of using it to advance one's financial or academic status, or as the promising avenue to avail oneself of the comforts of life, or as a haven to shelter oneself from the vagaries of life, such a person is involved in a dangerous trade of manipulation of self and the Church. It is like the man who marries a woman from a rich family in order to have access to their money and not because he loves her. He gets the woman and the money, and has some children. But his family life is always strained: he has money, popularity and mistresses all over the place, but he is happier when he is away from home. The thought of coming home is a nightmare, and when he does come, the atmosphere is full of tension because he is uncomfortable. Yet, he cannot run away from home, and he fears treating the wife badly or sending her away for he owes his richness to her family members. As can be seen, his original manipulative ploy turns out to be his manipulation of himself. The alternative before him is to convert and learn to love the woman as his wife, with or without money.

In the same way, those of us who entered the priesthood with wrong motives – which are conscious distortion – often succeed in getting what they desired; but they may remain profoundly unfulfilled or dissatisfied because the life they live is a lie, unless they undergo a restructuring of their original intention. Even when such persons did not make the values of the priesthood part of their original ideals, they are still not free psychologically, to live anyhow without paying the price. The reason is because there is more to life than getting money, positions of power and academic titles. This does not take time to become obvious. Again, it is an unrealistic expectation to hope to find shelter from life's problems in the priesthood, because the priesthood does not protect anyone from the problems of life nor is it a place to live a life of pleasure. These expectations have no basis in reality; they often come from the desires and needs of the individual.

It is also true that we may have the right motive in entering the priestly vocation but may have subconscious desires that are not only dissonant to the vocation but are also central in the motivational system. For instance, a person may have the good intention of becoming a priest in order to preach the Gospel and serve the people, but associates being a priest subconsciously with being an achiever. He becomes a priest, works hard and prays to be a bishop one day. Nothing is wrong with being a bishop, and someone has to be in that position. The only problem is that this desire forms a central aspect of this priest's need to achieve and to stand out among other persons. While this is his greatest aspiration as a priest, it may also constitute a great source of frustration and dissatisfaction in his life. A story was told of a monsignor who worked in the Vatican and did all he could to be made a bishop. He had worked his way from the time of ordination to the Vatican and hoped that even if he did not become the bishop of his home diocese, at least he would wear the red cap one day and display the golden ring – that would be the climax of his priestly and life ambitions. Unfortunately, he retired without becoming one. As a result, he became so sad and depressed. To cheer himself up, he bought for himself the bishop's ring, which he wore on certain occasions. But instead of feeling happier, he got more depressed and angry each time he put it on. His last years were full of sighs and regrets. He might not have known how strong his need to achieve was, and how it got constantly mixed up with his pure intention to serve like Christ rather than to be served. Though he served the Church well, he retired as a frustrated man constantly weighed down by the feeling that his life was irreparably lost. The priesthood rather than being a source of joy for him became a trap of danger, dissatisfaction and meaninglessness. For this reason, he could not relish his contributions to the Church, but felt his life was a waste; that it would have been better for him if he had not become a priest!

The situation is different for the priest who has become more aware of his subconscious needs and desires, how they manifest themselves in his daily life and makes effort to let Jesus win them over by His grace. Such a priest will continue to have needs and desires that will continue to mix up with his pure or good intentions, but he has learned to identify them when they show up and can always rely on the mercy and goodness of God consciously. He does his best to reaffirm in his life the priority of Jesus and the mission of the Church. This is also accompanied by more informed decisions and choices that enable him to live the values in which he believes.

As human beings, we carry our psychological needs and desires, and these constantly mix up with our good intentions so that, as Valles observes, there is "not a single action, even by the greatest of saints", which "is ever performed out of pure love of God"[6]. This bold acknowledgement of the human condition does not diminish the goodness of the actions of good and well-intentioned people and their honest efforts to live a good life. What is rather at stake is the importance of knowing the limitations of the human motivational system as expressed in the configurations of our individual personalities. This is a valid condition for human and vocational growth. 2

Valles, a Jesuit priest who lived in India for most of his life, wrote about how his subconscious needs mixed up with his pure intention of becoming a Jesuit priest[7]. He became aware of them as he challenged his deepest motivations in following Christ as a Jesuit priest on mission. First, he noticed he became a Jesuit because God called him and he was sure of it. His decision to be a religious was "a personal example of how God can make his own voice heard in the hearts of men with absolute authority and total exclusion of any doubt. If I had not joined, I would have felt guilty and considered myself a traitor for the rest of my life. And the underlying feeling was one of personal love for Christ"[8]. His intention was pure and his motive right. But as years went by and the demands of priestly life challenged his whole being, he became more aware of the external circumstances and other subconscious motives that got mixed up with his 'pure love of Christ': he had lost his father a few years before and was not sure of the future; secondly, he was in a Jesuit boarding school where the best students qualified to join the novitiate, and he was the best. To join the novitiate was a matter of prestige, and to become a Jesuit then in Spain was "an honour and a privilege, and a family which had a son in the Society improved its social standing"[9]; thirdly, there was the pressure of his Spiritual Father who would approach him "stealthily from behind and said in my ear with an underworld tone of voice: 'hear the voice of Christ from the cross, who commands you to follow him into the novitiate'"[10]. The presence of these subconscious motives did not render his vocation invalid nor do they mean that he was tricked into being a Jesuit priest. Rather, they indicate that his motive to be a Jesuit priest was a mixture of pure love of God and of these subconscious elements. God uses different circumstances to draw each person to himself.

Though Valles knew that God had brought him to this vocation through the conspiracy of the external circumstances and those needs and desires in him that he was not aware of then, he did not stop there: he struggled, through continuous self-knowledge, to know the workings of his heart and to identify these other motives in order to make decisions and choices that reflect more an ordering of his life towards God as a

Christian and as a Jesuit priest. The keyword here is awareness or self-knowledge and concrete decisions and actions based on that. It is not an easy struggle and, perhaps, it will last till the end of our life. That makes human, Christian, and vocational life a pilgrimage. Our joy as priests lies in this awareness that we are not yet finished; that the grace of God is operative in us as we make honest effort to subject our whole self and our desires and needs to the obedience of Jesus Christ. But Jesus has to be central in our lives in order to challenge these needs and desires and transform them. Hence, vocational maturity is a dynamic process of continuous submission to Jesus Christ and the values of the Gospel.

Between Our Limits and Our Ideals

What comes out clearly from the reflection so far is that there is a gap that exists between what each of us is at each moment and what we are called to be; between the ideals we struggle to live and our actual life-situations. But this gap is necessary because it describes well our human condition: it is a pilgrimage to fullness of life in God. It does not have to bring fear and discouragement or depression to us priests or seminarians; it enables us to see clearly the true nature of our struggles and the relevant factors involved in order to accept them, seek better working strategies of growing, and implore the grace of God more insistently. Secondly, the gap between who we are called to be and our real life-situations expresses the true experience of every priest that no one is completely made; that each one of us either moves toward or away from his self-fulfilment as each day passes. What is not negotiable in vocational and human growth is *not knowing* those aspects of our persons that obstruct or enable development.

Despite the gap that exists between the ideal and the real situation of our lives as priests, we can be joyful and fulfilled when we know our limitations and ambivalences, and make a sincere and conscious effort to grow and bring them steadily to the obedience of Jesus Christ, and resisting discouragement. I have become deeply convinced that when we look onto Christ who has called us despite our weaknesses, and advance towards deeper union with Him, through conscious efforts to live the values of the priestly life, we experience deep sense of meaning and direction. We may not succeed always and in all circumstances, but we are and should not be discouraged. We should not give up seeking greater acquisition of our vocational identity in Jesus Christ and in the Church.

Our psychological baggage constitutes the raw material upon which the grace of God works to bring about our transformation and that of the world. The real danger for us priests is to be unaware of what the raw material of our humanity consists of. Or, knowing it, we fail to accept and work on it. This situation can often lead us to aberrant behaviours that surprise us and the people. It can lead to different forms of inconsistent lifestyle some of which could be scandalous; it can lead to unnecessary dissipation of energy in a fruitless search for life, meaning, and fulfilment elsewhere. Thirdly, some of us can be frustrated and angry without knowing why we are so. Oftentimes, it is the people placed under our care that suffer for the consequences of this internal dissatisfaction. This is where the shadow side of our lives takes over and makes our lives and that of others miserable.

The essence of an immature priestly life is the hesitation to give oneself totally to God in love. It is comically expressed by B.M. Dolphin as a "Yes, but" response to God's call. "Such a person is like someone driving a car with the hand-brake partially on. The car can move, but only slowly and it cannot accelerate" [11]. This hesitation shows itself in forms of conscious and unconscious misinterpretations or convenient interpretations of the priestly vocation. This tendency to convenient interpretation indicates our ambivalence in relation to the values of the priesthood and point to the intrinsic ambiguities of our motivational system. I have noticed this hesitation many times in my own life. I take the life of prayer as an example. There are times I just would hesitate to have that precious hour with the Lord, despite my knowledge that the

Lord is the most important person in my life, and the center of my whole life. At times, the desire to love him is strong enough that being with him in prayer is easy. At other times, it is such a pain.

This hesitation makes growth in priestly vocation painful and difficult. I have therefore come to understand that the decision to live for God totally is not made once and for all because the counter-pull of weaknesses is always present. Lonergan clearly notes that "human authenticity is never some pure and serene and secure possession. It is ever a withdrawal from inauthenticity, and every successful withdrawal only brings to light the need for still further withdrawals"[12]. That is to say, we are never completely secured in our achieved maturity; the immature side of us is always present because we have personal desires and needs that seek to be gratified. Some of these personal desires and wants work against our sincere decision to give ourselves totally to God and to others.

For this reason, growth in the priestly vocation entails this "constant withdrawal from inauthenticity", the constant decision to live the priestly life fully according to the values of the priesthood; the constant decision to love Jesus above everything and to live according to the values of the gospel. The tension between what we are as priests and what we should be is always there. But we grow in our vocation and humanity each time we make decisions and choices that bring us closer to Jesus and promote the Church's mission in the world. When we grow in this manner, we can bring the hope and consolation of God to the people entrusted to our care and to the wounded conditions of our social order. As we grow, we gradually make what we should be to be what we *want* so that we experience some degree of integration in our personality. This is a deep source of satisfaction in the life of a priest. When I finished my studies in Rome, some priests adviced me to stay back and "make some money for yourself because Nigeria is tough". I knew that they loved me by making that suggestion. But I battled over it: what was the Lord asking of me? Would I be seeking my own pleasure by staying back? And staying back just to make money? I still recall kneeling before the Lord in the Blessed Sacrament in our college chapel muttering to myself amidst this confusion: "you have to go home. This is what is needed of you". After that decision, peace descended into my embattled heart. I left Italy for home with practically nothing. But it was a big decision that helped me in my relationship with God.

It is obvious to me that whenever our values, desires, needs, and wants as priests – especially those that contradict what our whole life stands for – prevail and control our lives so that obedience to Jesus Christ and the values of the Gospel become secondary in our lives, we have become dangerous leaders of God's people. In this disposition, our activities may actively work against the mission of the Church in the world. Here we can place those of our members who have become sexual predators or those who are driven by the thirst for power and domination that they can do anything possible to gain it and use it in a harmful way; the priests who devote their lives to acquiring wealth and comfort that they lose sense of what is right or wrong since every act that leads to money and comfort is permissible. Such priests could grow very insensitive to the condition of the people entrusted to them or even exploit them. When these types of priests are in great number, the values of the gospel and the mission of the Church are in serious danger. It is one of the greatest sources of loss of faith for a good number of Catholics. This is that situation wherein what should be light has turned into darkness and has the capacity to destroy persons and things.

This means that priestly life can lead both to light and to darkness, depending on the personality of the priest and the readiness of the priests themselves to engage in personal and vocational growth. The dialectic between light and darkness in the life of priests is a permanent condition in the Church, as long as priests are human beings. However, it can be handled better if bishops and those in the formation of priests take it into consideration and make effort to reduce the number of persons who have the high potentiality of being harmful to themselves and to the Church. But most importantly, it belongs to each of us to examine ourselves and see how we experience and handle this tension, for on it depends largely our experience of fulfilment as priests. I feel strongly that the management of this tension should not be understood in terms of the wilful effort to root out all our weaknesses. Such wilfulness never works; it can only lead to unhelpful self-preoccupation. Rather, it consists in our continuous openness to the grace of God by which we are enabled to choose to please Him in every moment of choice in our lives. As Henri Nouwen rightly says: the basic question is whether the Living God is really alive in the heart of the priest!

Epilogue: God is Faithful

As I come to the end of this writing, my eyes are soaked in tears and my heart melted with the feelings of gratitude to God for his tremendous love. It is the love that brought us into the world. It is the love that brought us into the Church, the Bride of Christ. It is the same love that brought us into the priesthood and is sustaining us through the joys and trials that we continue to experience. I sing of the faithfulness of this love. Whatever I have reflected on, researched upon and written, shrink before the amazing experience of this God who calls us in Jesus Christ, through the Holy Spirit, in the Church. This love constitutes the starting point and the end of our journey. As priests, we respond to this love with love, and give ourselves wholeheartedly to Him and to the Church, where God has positioned us. May this God whose love is everlasting lead us more deeply into the mystery of our priestly calling so that we can savour the height and the depth of it, to the glory of His name. Amen.

Notes

Chapter One

[1] For a detailed study on this, see C.U. Okeke (2006). *The Future of Catholic Priesthood in Igboland: Dangers and Challenges*. Nimo, Nigeria, Rex Charles & Patrick Ltd.

[2] *The Oxford English Reference Dictionary,* (1996) Oxford, New York, Oxford University Press, 2nd ed.

[3] A.S. Reber (1985). *Dictionary of Psychology*, Penguin Books.

[4] R.J. Campbell (1996). *Psychiatric Dictionary*. Oxford, New York, 7th ed. Oxford University Press, 7th ed.

[5] C.B. Daly (1994). Preface to B. Mcgregor & T. Norris (Eds.).*The Formation Journey of the Priest. Exploring "Pastoral Dabo Vobis"* Dublin, 8.

[6] John Paul II (1990). Post-Synodal Apostolic Exhortation, *Pastores Dabo Vobis*, 11; henceforth, *PDV*.

[7] Second Vatican Council, Dogmatic Constitution on the Church, *Lumen Gentium*, 21 November 1964, 10 & 28, henceforth, *LG*; Decree on the Ministry and Life of Priests, *Presbyterorum Ordinis*, 7 December 1963, 2; henceforth, *PO*. Cf. also *PDV*, 12.

[8] *LG*, 2-4.

[9] *LG*, 1.

[10] The Church is the universal sacrament of salvation and so is charged with the mission of bringing salvation to all men. Cf. *LG*, 1, 3, 48.

[11] B. Kloppenberg (1974). *The Ecclesiology of Vatican II*, 14.

[12] B.M. Nolan (1992). What Difference Does Priestly Ordination Make? In J.M. Murphy (Ed). *New Beginnings in Ministry*. Dublin, 129.

[13] *PDV*, 12; Cf. also B.M. Nolan (1992), 128-129.

[14] *PO*, 2.

[15] *LG*, 10.

[16] *PO*, 2.

[17] Synod of Bishops *Ultimis Temporibus*, 30 November 1967, I, 3; henceforth, *UT*.

[18] *PO*, 2; *PDV*, 21.

[19] *PDV*, 15.

[20] *PO*, 12.

[21] Second Vatican Council, Dogmatic Constitution on the Sacred Liturgy, *Sacrosanctum Concilium*, 4 December 1963, 33; henceforth, *SC*. Cf. also *LG*, 10, 28; *PO*, 2, 13; *UT*, I, 4; Congregation for the Doctrine of the Faith, *Inter Insigniores*, 15 October 1976, 5. Henceforth, *Inter Insigniores*; John Paul II, Encyclical Letter, *Ecclesia De Eucharistia*, on the Eucharist in its Relationship to the Church, 17 April 2003, 29.

[22] This is especially manifest in the eucharistic celebration where the priest offers the sacrificial victim in his own name and in the name of the whole Church. Cf. *SC*, 33; *LG*, 10, 28; *PO*, 2.

[23] A. Favale (1990). Identità Teologica del Presbitero, *Lateranum* 56, 441-483, 472. (Translation supplied)

[24] "Without personal holiness it will be possible to hold the office of a priest, and to minister the sacraments validly, but the fruitfulness of the ministry will be compromised". A. Dulles (1997). *The Priestly Office. A Theological Reflection* . New York, Mahwah, Paulist Press, 65.

[25] *PO*, 3.

[26] Cf. A. Favale (1990), 457; P. Vanzan (1992). *Pastores dabo vobis*: Chiavi di Lettura Ecclesiologico-Tinitaria, Cristologica e Pastorale, *Civiltà Cattolica* 143/4, 233-343, 353-361, 235.

[27] *UT*, I, 4.

[28] *LG*, 21, 28; *PO*, 2.

[29] *PO*, 5.

[30] *PO*, 4.

[31] F. Wulf – *al* (1989). Commentary on the Decree [on the Ministry and Life of Priests). In H. Vormgrimler (Ed). *Commentary on the Documents of Vatican II*, New York, 224.

[32] Ibid., 223.

[33] *LG*, 10.

[34] *PDV*, 14; *PO*, 2; *LG*, 18.

[35] *Catechism of the Catholic Church*, 1547 (henceforth, *CCC*).

[36] *LG*, 24; *CCC*, 1551.

[37] T. Lane (1993). *A Priesthood in Tune. Theological Reflections on the Ministry*. Dublin, 103.

[38] *PDV*, 16. These two dimensions of the priestly identity should always be held together. But the fundamental dimension is that of the union between the priest and Christ. Cf. Congregation for the Clergy, *The Priest, Pastor and Leader of the Parish Community*, 4 August 2002, 10-11; P. Laghi (1993). Pastores dabo vobis. Presentazione, *Seminarium* 32, 505-517, 506-509. See also D.M. Buechelein (2000). The Sacramental Identity of the Ministerial Priesthood: "*In Persona Christi*". In *Priests for a New Millennium*. Washington, D.C. United States Catholic Conference, 37-42.

[39] Second Vatican Council, Decree on the Training of Priests, *Optatum Totius*, 28 October 1965, 4; henceforth, *OT*.

[40] K.B. Osborne (1988). *Priesthood: A History of the Ordained Ministry in the Roman Catholic Church*. New York, Mahwah, 334.

[41] Ibid.

[42] Congregation For Evangelisation Of Peoples (1989). *Pastoral Guide for Diocesan Priests*, Vatican City, 2.

[43] *PDV*, Chapter III.

[44] A. Dulles (1997), 63.

[45] F.Wulf – *al* (1989), 268.

[46] *PO*, 2, 12; *PDV*, 21.

[47] *PDV*, 16.

[48] P. Laghi (1993), 508 (Translation supplied)

[49] J. Ratzinger (1996). *Zur Gemeinschaft gerufen: Kirche heute verstehen*. Eng. Trans. *Called to Communion*. By A. Walker, San Francisco, Ignatius Press, 114-115.

[50] *PO*, 12. "In particular, the greater or lesser degree of the holiness of the minister has a real effect on the proclamation of the word, the celebration of the sacraments and the leadership of the community in charity". *PDV*, 25.

[51] H. Nouwen (1989). *In the Name of Jesus*. Darton, Longman, and Todd, 10.

[52] Ibid., 11.

[53] J. Vanoosting (2002). Vocation Education, *America*, 187/1, 8-11, 10.

[54] J.B.C. Okorie (1995). *Social Interest, Lifestyle, Stress and Job Satisfaction of Nigerian Catholic Priests*. Unpublished Doctoral Dissertation, University of San Francisco. However, it turned out that because of this limitation, the research did not yield very significant results.

[55] T. Costello (2002). *Forming a Priestly Identity*. Rome, Gregorian University Press, 182.

[56] As Walter Magni (2001) emphatically notes: "Any fulfilment that is rigidly centred on the self, such as the dynamic of self-realization would suppose, basically denies the profound and singular truth of the christian vocation in its primordial characteristic of gift of self, an offering and a gift of one's life". Giovani e Coscienza Vocazionale, *Palestra del Clero*, 5-6, 389-407, 399. [Translation supplied] George Niederauer (1999) suspects that taking the priesthood as a career of self-realization is behind some clericalist attitude of some priests. He cites the example of a newly ordained priest who had to remind a religious woman who called him by his name: "'Call me Father! I worked long and hard for that!' That smells to me of privatisation of the priestly vocation, the noisome transformation of a call from God into some kind of ecclesiastical MBA". See his A Ministerial Spirituality. In K.S. Smith (Ed). *Priesthood in the Modern World*. Franklin, Wisconsin, Sheed & Ward, 74. Such attitude smacks of a careerist mentality where one has made it by the sole force of one's will power and determination.

[57] *PDV*, 44; J. Ratzinger (1996), 115-116. B.J.F. Lonergan (1971) affirms the same thing when he notes that "man

achieves authenticity in self-transcendence" and that he "is his true self in as much as he is self-transcending". *Method in Theology*. Toronto, University of Toronto Press, 104, 357.

[58] L.M. Rulla (1986). *Anthropology of the Christian Vocation*. Rome, Gregorian University Pressl, vol. 1, 267. Henceforth, *ACV*, I.

[59] *PDV*, 36.

[60] *PDV*, 36; *Inter Insigniores*, 6.

[61] J. Ratzinger (1996), 115.

[62] John Paul II, Address to the Plenary Meeting of the Congregation for the Clergy, 23 Novmber 2001, 215.

[63] T. Costello (2002) 109.

[64] *Inter Insigniores*, 6.

[65] *PDV*, 35.

[66] T. Costello (2002), 186.

[67] "Some currents in contemporary culture regard interior virtue, mortification and spirituality as forms of introspection, alienation, or of egoism which are incapable of understanding the problems of the world and of people. In some instance, this has led to a multifarious image of the priest: it ranges from the sociologist to the therapist, from the politician to the manager. It has even led to the idea of the 'retired' priest. In this context, it has to be recalled that the priest is a full-time bearer of an ontological consecration". Congregation for the Clergy, *The Priest, Pastor and Leader*, 11.

[68] *UT*, I, 5.

[69] R.M. Gula, (1996). *Ethics in Pastoral Ministry*. New York, Mahwah, 13.

[70] H.L. Wilensky (1964). The Professionalization of Everyone, *American Journal of Sociology* , 70, 137-158, 137.

[71] Ibid.,139.

[72] R.M. Gula (1996), 13-14.

[73] See the summary of these criteria from different studies in T.M. Gannon (1971). Priest/Minister: Profession or Non-Profession, *Review of Religious Research* , 12, 66-79, 67-68; T. Costello (2002), 185-186.

[74] Ibid., 67. For Wilensky, these two criteria will entail first, that the job of a professional is technical, that is, "based on systematic knowledge or doctrine acquired only through long prescribed training"; secondly, that the professional adheres to a set of professional norms. H.L. Wilensky (1964), 140.

[75] Ibid., 68.

[76] T. Costello (2002). 186.

[77] T.M. Gannon (1971), 73. The identity of the priest belongs to the order of faith experienced and lived in the Church. It can only be understood, lived, and deepened within this context and not outside of it. Cf. A. Favale (1990), 476; G. Danneels (1994), 29.

[78] T.M. Gannon (1971), 74.

[79] T. Costello (2002) 186. J.W. Carroll (1985) suggests that in order for the professional model to be applied to priestly ministry, it needs to be reconceptualised. It will consider "the kind of professional competence required for the clergy role, not in terms of specific skills but rather of a method for ministry that overcomes the liabilities of technical rationality". For example, it will involve the capacity of the priest to bring his knowledge of God and of the Christian tradition to bear on the situations he encounters. Formation of priests will have "to be oriented towards helping students to clarify their personal vision of God through a firm grounding in the Christian tradition and to do so in such a way that they develop expertise in its application to the concrete situations of ministerial practice". See his article, The Professional Model of Ministry, *Theological Education*, 21, 7-48, 28-38. Even this reconceptualisation still appears to lay undue emphasis on expert management of concrete situations. The Church rather gives primacy to the *being* of the priest from which all he does and the way he does them derive. Jesus approached every situation he encountered from the very depth of his identity as the beloved Son of God who has been commissioned to bring the Father's love to humanity. The appropriation of priestly identity comes first.

[80] T.M. Gannon (1971), 76.

[81] Synod of Bishops, *De Sacerdotibus Formandis in Hodiernis Adiuntis. Instrumentum Laboris*, 15 July 1990, 44.

[82] *PDV*, 57.

[83] D. Coletti (1992). Il Seminario Maggiore, *Seminarium* 32, 561– 574, 571. (Translation supplied)

[84] R. Rohr (2002). Beyond Crime and Punishment, *Sojourners* July-August, 26-27, 27, 59.

[85] P. Laghi (1992:509) holds that the spirituality of "pastoral charity" specific to the priesthood is appropriate because, being the sacrament of Christ, the priest cannot but integrate all the elements of his person and ministry around the figure of the good shepherd who gives his life for his sheep.

[86] *PDV*, 23. Citing Pope John Paul II's Homily at the Eucharistic Adoration, Seoul, Oct. 7, 1989. (Emphasis is mine).

[87] *PDV*, 21.

[88] *PDV*, 21.

[89] F.Wulf, - *al* (1989), 223-224.

[90] *PO*, 9, 14; *PDV*, 22, 23.

[91] *PO*, 4, 6, 9.

[92] *PO*, 6; *PDV*, 22.

[93] *PDV*, 22; *PO*, 6.

[94] *PO*, 15.

[95] *PDV*, 23.

[96] P. Laghi (1992), 510-511.

[97] F. Rypar (1992). La *pastores dabo vobis* alla luce del Pensiero conciliare sul sacerdozio e la formazione sacerdotale, *Seminarium* 31, 530-549, 539.

[98] G. Danneels (1994), 33-34. See also N. Cachia (1997). *The Image of the Good Shepherd as a Source for the Spirituality of the Ministerial Priesthood*. S.T.D. Dissertation, Pontifical Gregorian University, Rome, 314-317.

[99] *ACV*, I, 287.

[100] T. Costello (2002), 186.

[101] A relevant study in this connection was carried out in the United States on religious priests, sisters, and brothers who were professionally trained. The researchers found out that "the more highly educated among the population experience

lower role clarity as religious". D. Nygren & M. Ukeritis (1992). Future of Religious Orders in the United States: Research Executive Summary, *Origins*, 22, 258-272, 263.

[102] Anthony de Mello (1990). *Contact with God. Retreat Conferences*. Gujarat India, Anand Press, 14-15.

[103] Empirical evidence demonstrates that such over-identification with role occurs in those individuals in whom subconscious needs are prevalent to such a degree as to conduce them to seek their own identity in such roles rather than in being priests. Cf. L.M.Rulla, J.Riddick & F. Imoda (1988). *Entering and Leaving Vocation*. Rome, Gregorian University Press, 233-247. Henceforth, *ELV*. See also *ACV*, I, 405-407. These are the people identified in the research of E.C. Kennedy and V.J. Heckler (1972) as underdeveloped priests whose sense of identity rests heavily on the "supports of the role characteristics of the priesthood". *The Catholic Priest in the United States. Psychological Investigations*. Washington D.C., 89.

[104] Cf. D. Ranson (2002). Priest: Public, Personal and Private, *The Furrow* 53/54, 219-227, 220; T. Costello, (1992). The Use of Psychology as an Aid in Priestly Formation, *Seminarium* 32, 629-636, 633.

[105] M. Drennan (1994). The Word of God: The Radical Source of Christian Formation. In B. Mcgregor & T. Norris (Eds.). *The Formational Journey of the Priest. Exploring "Pastores Dabo Vobis*. Dublin, 56-58. See also C.B. Okolo (1993). Priestly Formation and the Challenge of Christianity: Nigerian Situation Revisited. In the Symposium on Priestly Formation in the Spirit of *Pastores Dabo Vobisi* of John Paul II, Imezi-Owa, Enugu, Nigeria, 10. (Original Copy)

[106] T. Costello (2002), 183; B. Winters (1995). *Priest as Leader: The Process of the Inculturation of a Spiritual-Theological Theme of Priesthood in a United States Context*. S.T.D. Dissertation, Pontifical Gregorian University, Rome, 159; G. Weigel (2002). *The Courage to be Catholic: Crisis, Reform, and the Future of the Church*. New York, Basic Books, 23-24.

[107] A.T. Ukwuoma (2000). *Being a Priest in a Changing Society. Psycho-social Analysis of the Nigerian Experience*. Kearney NE, 20.

[108] That is why the suggestion of Sweetser, that the Church be seen as a management concept and the ministers managers, seems to misstate the question. Cf. T.P. Sweetser (1992). Parish Leadership versus Parish Management, *Human Development* 13, 13-15, 13-14. The Church understands the priest to be a leader and not a manager. Leadership itself is a more embracing concept than management. For details, see also A. D'Souza (1989). *Leadership. A Trilogy on Leadership and Effective Management*. Nairoi, Kenya, Paulines Pulications Africa, 23-29.

[109] *ACV*, I, 365.

[110] T. Costello 2002), 236.

Chapter Two

[1] For a detailed analysis of the dialectic between the prevailing world order and the new world order announced by Jesus, see R. Rohr & J.B. Feister (1996). *Jesus' Plan for a New World. The Sermon on the Mount*. Mumbai, St. Paul.

[2] B.J.F. Lonergan (1971), 35.

[3] Balthasar (1993) makes an important remark that could be applied to the subject of our discussion. That we have died and been raised with Christ is a fact. This is an indicative. But there is also the imperative: that each man hears and acts upon this fact. (See his *Kennt uns Jesus – Kennen wir ihm?* Eng. Trans. By G. Harrison, *Does Jesus Know Us? Do We Know Him?* San Francisco, Ignatius, 40. The indicative relates to the objective aspect of the priestly identity, the intellectual definition and knowledge of this new vision of life, and the imperative relates to the subjective aspect in which the individual applies himself to being that which is there objectively.

[4] *LG*, 40.

[5] *PDV*, 27. Cf. B. Winters (1995), 140-142.

[6] P. Lane (1994). The Religious and Diocesan Priest: A Mutual Enrichment. In B. Mcgregor & T. Norris (Eds.)*The Formational Journey of the Priest* . Dublin, 49.

[7] There is the tendency among some priests to see the evangelical counsels only in their pastoral usefulness. For such priests, the counsels are meant to make the priest free to carry out his duties. This attitude can easily degenerate into a selective interpretation of the counsels themselves. But the counsels have their basis in Christ. They express the dynamism of the life of Christ himself. Thus, their fundamental thrust is in the imitation of the life of Christ which is to be manifested concretely in pastoral work.

[8] F. Wulf - *al* (1989), 223.

[9] *PO*, 14; *PDV*, 28.

[10] *PO*, 15.

[11] Vanoosting (2002:10) affirms that, "Vocation focuses on obedience, accountability, and faithfulness to the caller. Vocation demands life-ordering disciplines to ensure responsiveness and also requires silence, in order to be attentive to the caller".

[12] *PO*, 15.

[13] *PO*, 15. In *Pastores Dabo Vobis*, these two dimensions of priestly obedience are further specified in three ways: priestly obedience is *apostolic*, that is, the priest should love the Church and the hierarchy; it is *communitarian*, that is, it demands cooperation with the members of the presbyterium; and third, it is *pastoral*, that is, the availability which the pastoral ministry demands. The apostolic and communitarian aspects of obedience can both come under obedience to the constituted authority while the pastoral dimension restates the readiness of the priest to spend himself and be spent for the people of God. Thus, the teaching of *Pastores dabo vobis* is consistent with that of the Second Vatican Council though this further specification adds to the clarity of the doctrine.

[14] F. Wulf – *al* (1989), 278.

[15] *PO*, 14.

[16] These two classes of persons in relation to gospel-obedience has been described well by Maloney in these words: "A fear-ridden individual who has to be protected from all decision-making by the strong superior, is not fully human and therefore not fully Christian. Another person who wants to do his or her 'own thing' all the time has lost the sense of the Cross, of being an imitator of Christ ...." See F.J. Maloney (1980). *Disciples and Prophets*. New York, Crossroad, 125.

[17] L. Sperry (1991). Neurotic Personalities in Religious Settings, *Human Development* 12, 12-17.

[18] *PO*, 16. Cf. also Paul VI, Encyclical Letter on Priestly Celibacy,*Sacerdotalis Caelibatus*, 24 June 1967,13.

[19] *PO*, 29. This understanding of priestly celibacy, as essentially founded on love for Christ and Christ's Church rather than on mere renunciation of sexual pleasure, prevailed at the 8th synod of bishops. Cf. G. Caprile (1992). Il Celibato Sacerdotale al Sinodo dei Vescovi 1990, *Civiltà Cattolica* 143/4, 488-501, 489-490. It is radically rooted in the spousal relationship of the priest with the Church. Cf. F. Rypar (1992), 539-540.

[20] *PDV*, 29.

[21] Paul VI, *Sacerdotalis Caelibatus*, 24.

[22] See the argument of I. McQuillan (1992) Celibacy and the Faithful, *The Furrow* 43, 414. The Church does not see it as a mere discipline for pastoral efficiency; it is a gift of God which she considers as conforming to the nature of the priesthood. Thus John McAreavey (1994) argues that the starting point of the Church's understanding of priestly celibacy is that it is a charism. And if it is a charism it is "a supernatural gift bestowed by the Holy Spirit for building up the Body of Christ. Hence a charism is not an aptitude or a skill which a person can acquire by habit or practice. It is given by God and God does not take back a gift once given". See his Celibacy: A Gift of Pastoral Charity. In In B. Mcgregor & T. Norris (Eds.)*The Formational Journey of the Priest* . Dublin, 101. Even if it is a discipline, priestly celibacy is rooted in Christ in whose person

the priest lives and ministers. For more detail on the related difficulties from this view point, Cf. C.B. Daly (1994), 13.

[23] C. Gallaher & T.L. Vandenberg (1989). *The Celibacy Myth. Loving for Life*. New York, 117.

[24] H. Flynn (1990). Celibacy: A Way to Love, *Origins* 20/19, 302-304, 303.

[25] J. Riddick (1984). *Treasures in Earthen Vessels*. New York, Alba House, 51.

[26] Kiesling (1978). *Celibacy, Prayer and Friendship. A Making-Sense-Out-Of-Life Approach*. New York, 35; G. Weigel (2002), 159-160.

[27] A. Grabner-Haider, *Letters to a Young Priest from a Laicised Priest*. California, 48.

[28] Cf. G. Caprile (1992), 491; B.M. Kieley (1999). Formation in Chastity. The Needs and Requirements. In L. Gormally (Ed.). *Issues for a Catholic Bioethic*, London, 134-147, 140. The question of Hoban (1992:495) s therefore unfortunate and misleading: "If the pleasures of sex have been acknowledged, albeit reluctantly, in the new theology of marriage, whither compulsory celibacy?". Cf. his What are we at? *The Furrow* 43, 491-496, 495.

[29] For example, Paul VI expressed in *Sarcedotalis Caelibatus* that "we consider that the present law of celibacy should today continue to be firmly linked to the ecclesiastical ministry". This statement is to be found in no. 14.

[30] Ibid. no. 15.

[31] K.B. Osborn (1988), 341.

[32] F.J. Maloney (1980), 112.

[33] Ibid.

[34] Ibid., 113.

[35] Ibid.

[36] Ibid., 114.

[37] *PO*, 17.

[38] *PDV*, 30.

[39] *PO*, 17; *PDV*, 30; *OT*, 9; *Code of Canon Law*, canon 282. In the present situation of the African people, such scandals could be seen in the life of the Church leaders and religious

men and women. It is visible in the prestigious buildings that fly in the face of the hard reality of African people; the fact that priests and religious men and women are seen as belonging to the affluent class of the society and of the Church; in the general conviction of many African Christians that going into the priesthood or the religious life is a rise in the social scale. Cf. A. Shorter (1999). *Religious Poverty in Africa*. Nairobi, Paulines Publications for Africa, 8-10.

[40] *PDV*, 30.

[41] "An over-attachment to material things, to people, to places, and a style of life that lacks simplicity, points to finding a false sense of security in those, rather than in the Lord. Indications of this can be quite evident, as to where one's heart is. Current models of cars, styles of dress, can take on undue significance, as examples". M. Drennan (1994). Special Issues in Human Formation. In B. Mcgregor & T. Norris (Eds.)*The Formational Journey of the Priest* . Dublin, 87.

[42] *PO*, 17.

[43] *PO*, 3.

[44] *PO*, 3.

Chapter Three

[1] See C.U. Okeke (2007). *I am Married but Lonely: Why?* Nimo, Nigeria, Rex Charles and Patrick Ltd.

[2] R.S. Reber (1985).

[3] L. von Bertalanffy (1968). *General Systems Theory*. New York, George Braziller, 214.

[4] E. Easwaran, *Original Goodness: On the Beatitudes*, 23-24.

[5] D. Power (1998). *A Spiritual Theology of the Priesthood*. Edinburgh, T & T Clark, 69.

[6] C.G. Valles (1992). *The Art of Choosing*. 2nd ed. Anand India, Anand Press 23.

[7] Ibid., 26-37. I single this one out for detailed presentation. The other two important decisions in his life include his decision to accept to go to India for mission, and his choice of living with poor Hindu families in Ahmedabad, begging

hospitality from house to house and sharing their life in everything, and from there going for his lectures in the college.

[8] Ibid., 26.

[9] Ibid., 27. This situation could, in certain ways, reflect well the current situation of the vocation to the priesthood and the religious life in certain parts of the world today where it is an honour to be a priest or a religious.

[10] Ibid., 28.

[11] B.M. Dolphin (1994). Human Formation: A Basis of Priestly Formation. In B. Mcgregor & T. Norris (Eds.)*The Formational Journey of the Priest* . Dublin, 79. Such a person, for C. O'Dwyer (2000:201) is "like a ship that is aground and fixed in place". See her *Imagining One's Future*. Rome, Gregorian University Press. W. Magni (2001:399) refers to it as "unconscious vocational unwillingness" which cripples young people from deciding to give themselves gratuitously to the vocation. Cf. Giovani e coscienza vocazionale, *Palestra del Clero* 5-6, 389-407. [Translation supplied] For a detailed philosophical analysis of this problem, see A. Scola, *Gesù. Destino dell'Uomo*. Torino, San Paolo, chapter 5.

[12] B.J. F. Lonergan (1971), 110. For a detailed analysis of this problem, see T. Healy (1997). La Sfida dell'Autotrascendenza. In F. Imoda (Ed.). *Antropologia Interdisciplinare e Formazione* , Bologna, Edizione Dehoniane Bologna, 133-135.

www.ingramcontent.com/pod-product-compliance
Lightning Source LLC
Chambersburg PA
CBHW032036040426
42449CB00007B/912